The Kindle Fire HDX User Guide

2015 Edition

By

Charles Tulley

Table of Contents

Table of Contents	1
Getting Started	**4**
Fresh Out of the Box	4
Connecting Your HDX	6
The Basics	**11**
Navigation	11
Sleeping	12
Notifications	12
Quick Settings	14
The Mayday Button & Amazon Assist	16
Charging	19
Restart	20
Volume Settings	21
Headphones	21
Screen Brightness	22
The Navigation Bar	22
The Carousel	24
Turning On/Off Recommendations	26
The Home Screen	28
The Options Bar	30
Disabling Special Offers	31
Favoriting Items	32
The Navigation Panel	32
Search	35
Connecting to Your Kindle Fire HDX	**39**
Wi-Fi Connections	39
Social Media Connections	41
Bluetooth	42
Data Transfers & Digital Content	**45**
USB Data Transfer	45
Email Data Transfer	46
Amazon Cloud Drive Sync	47
Clipping Articles	48
Transferring Other Digital Content	49
Using the HDX Keyboard	**51**
Keyboard Basics	51
Tap Input	53
Swype Input	53
The Kindle Fire HDX Browser	**56**
Silk Browser Basics	56

Advanced Silk Settings 58
Buying & Reading Books **61**
Purchasing Books 61
Reading Books 64
Whispersync 67
Using Apps **68**
Purchasing Apps 68
Email & Calendar **72**
Email Account Setup 72
Remove Email Account 74
Change Email Account Settings 75
TV, Video, Audiobooks & Music **76**
Buying/Renting TV & Movies 76
Finding Amazon Prime Videos 77
Music & Audiobooks 78
Taking & Editing Pictures & Videos **80**
Photo/Video Basics 80
Taking Pictures/Videos 81
Photo Editing 82
Advanced Settings, Tips & Tricks **84**
My Account 85
Help 85
Parental Controls 86
Device 86
Wireless 87
Applications 88
Notifications & Quiet Time 89
Display & Sounds 90
Keyboards 91
Accessibility 92
Security 93
Legal & Compliance 94
Tips & Tricks **95**
Reset to Factory Defaults 95
Side Loading Apps 95
Viewing Adobe Flash Content 97
Taking Screenshots 97
More Tips & Tricks 97
Physical Care of Your New Kindle Fire HDX **98**
Food & Drink 98
Cleaning the Screen & Body 98
Watch the Temperature 98
That's All, Folks! **100**

Getting Started

Fresh Out of the Box

When you first pull your Kindle Fire HDX out of the box, there are a few things you'll need to do before you can get started using it. First, pull off that plastic sleeve that it comes in, and retrieve the USB cable and power adapter (if included). Your HDX should come pre-charged to some degree (mine came around 60% charged) but it's a good idea to plug it in and charge it fully while you set things up. The charging port is a micro-USB port on the bottom edge of the device, as seen when you hold it in portrait mode with the camera on your left-hand side. (The charging port is angled upward and is near the power button on the bottom back of the device, which you can see below.)

If you've had a Kindle Fire HD, you'll notice some stark differences between the HD and HDX in terms of the device's physical appearance. Instead of having a power button and volume buttons on the top edge of the device, the three buttons are now on the *back* of the device. Flip your HDX around and look at the back, and it'll look something like this:

Notice that there is a pair of buttons (volume buttons) at one end and a single button (power button) at the opposite end. When holding your HDX in portrait mode, the way it's meant to be held is with the volume buttons at the top and power button at the bottom, so that the camera on the front is on your left-hand side. You can hold it pretty much however you want, though, since the device will change the screen orientation to fit however its currently being held.

Okay, so now that you know where the buttons are, let's get things started! Go ahead and press the power button and wait for the HDX to boot for the first time. Once it finishes booting, you should see the unlock screen that will resemble this:

Use your finger to slide the lock icon to the left, and you'll be presented with a language selection screen:

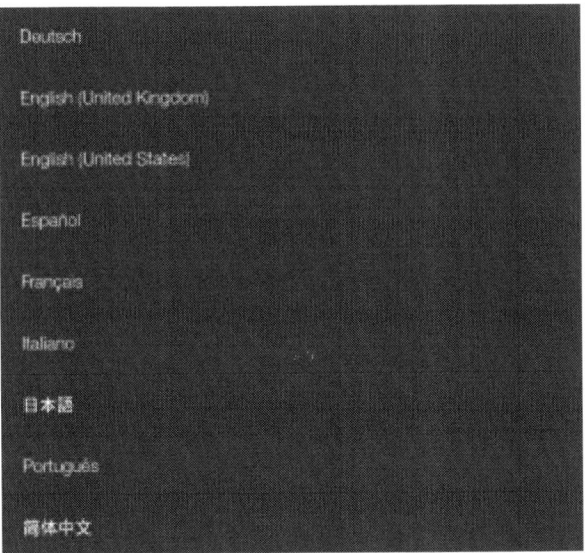

I'll be assuming that you chose **English (United States)** for the remainder of this guide book, so go ahead and tap on that selection, then tap the **Continue** button that appears below the language choices. The next section will cover your initial Wi-Fi setup, which is important for both registering your HDX and for getting online.

Connecting Your HDX

After choosing a language to use on your HDX, you'll see this screen:

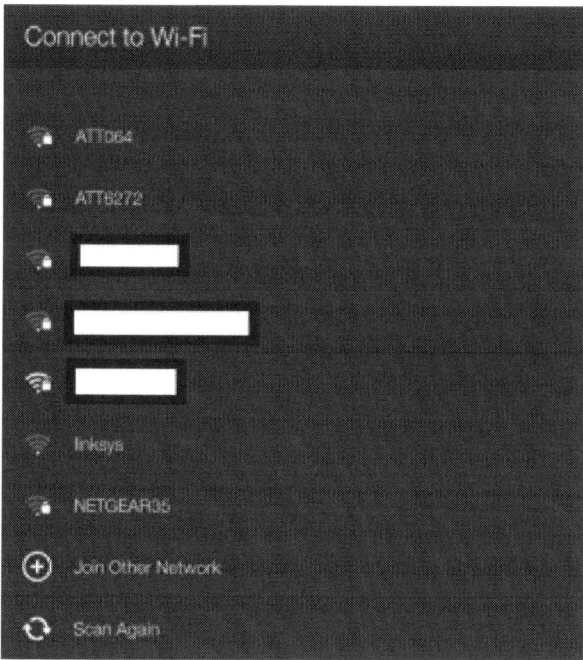

Connecting to a wireless network is how you'll be able to browse the web, download apps, access your Amazon account and a lot more. Go ahead and tap on your wireless network name in the list, and a popup will appear like below (I've blanked out some of my network information for privacy purposes):

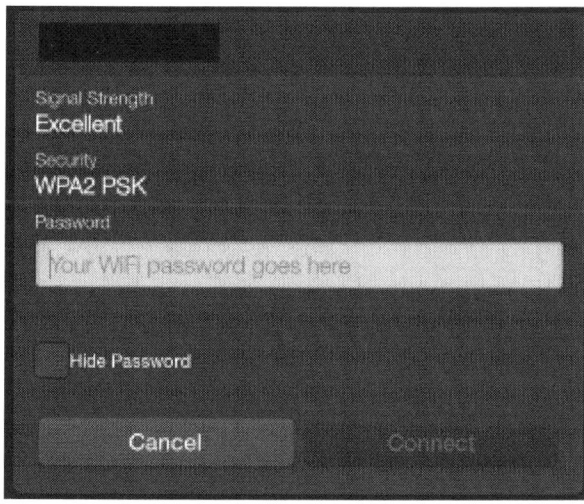

If your Wi-Fi network is secured, you'll be asked to type in the password using the on-screen keyboard that appears. Tap out the password, then tap **Connect** in the popup. Once your HDX connects, you'll be asked to confirm that you want to register the HDX to the Amazon account you purchased it with:

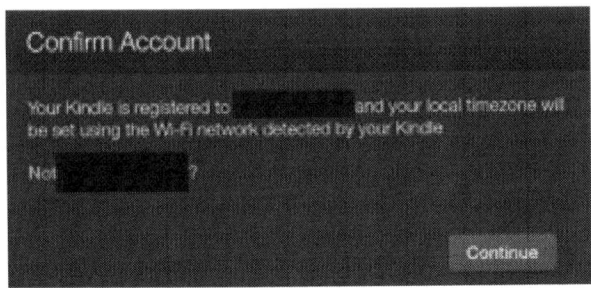

This registration can be changed by tapping **Not <Your Name>** and entering in the Amazon account information of the person you wish to register it to. If, however, you want to keep the registration information (I suspect most people will want to do this) then just tap **Continue**. If you purchased your HDX at a physical store, or something went wrong with the automatic registration, you'll be prompted to enter your Amazon account information to manually register it. Just type out your Amazon email and password as prompted and you'll be good to go.

Once you confirm the registration status, you might be asked to download a software update, and you might run into a connection issue like I did when I first powered it on:

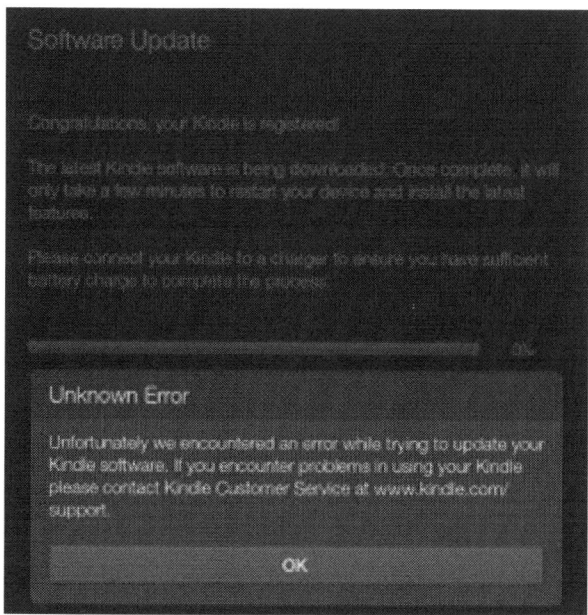

Don't worry if you see this; just tap **OK** and we'll try manually updating the software later in this guide book. If an update is available and is downloaded, you may be asked to restart your HDX after the download is complete. Go ahead and do this, then we'll be ready to move on to the next step:

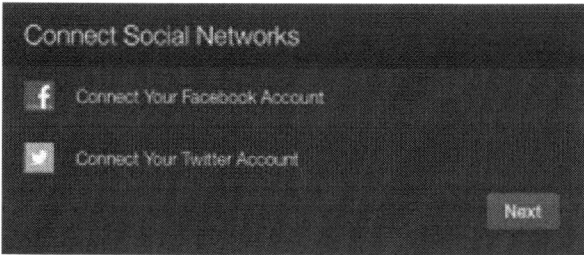

Like other steps in this setup process, you can choose to defer the setup of social networks until a later point in time—or never, if you prefer. To connect your Facebook and Twitter accounts to your HDX during the setup, though, tap on the **Connect Your <Social> Account** for Facebook and/or Twitter and fill out the information as you see below:

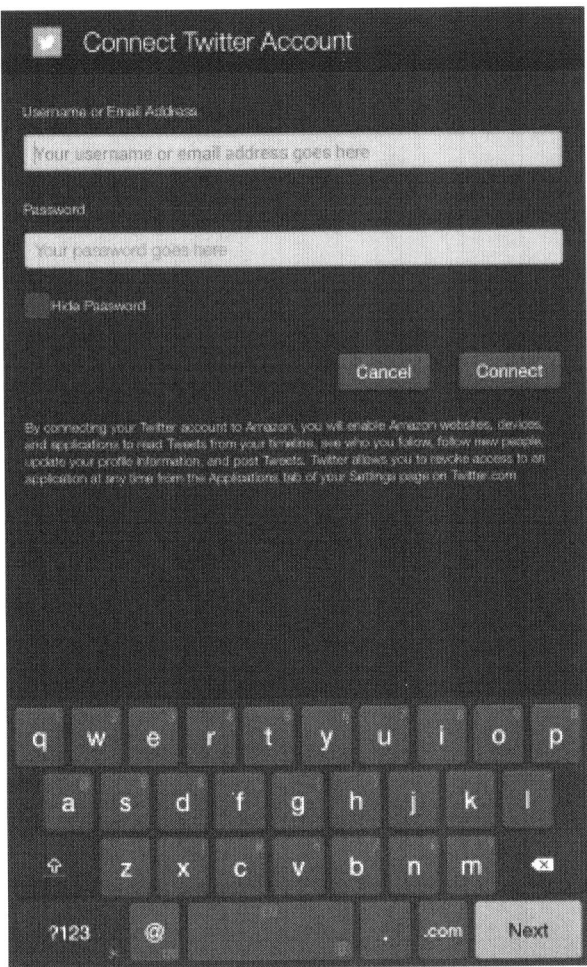

Once you connect your Facebook/Twitter accounts (or don't, as the case may be) tap the **Next** button to proceed to a quick overview of how to use your Kindle Fire HDX. This process is mandatory and I highly advise you to read it over carefully, even though I'll be going over the information contained in it later in this guide book.

The Basics

WOW! The Kindle Fire HDX is *incredibly* different than the Kindle Fire HD, yet similar, too! Let's get started by looking at some of the basics you'll need to know when you use the Kindle Fire HDX every day. Afterwards, we'll move into some advanced areas, including advanced settings, tips, tricks and more.

Navigation

Your HDX was designed from the ground up to be simple and easy to use. With mere swipes and taps from your fingers, you can navigate around through the HDX's different pages, opening apps, browsing web pages, reading books and watching videos. Before we can start doing that, though, there are a few things you'll need to remember when navigating through your HDX.

First off is the Home button. Whenever you see an icon that looks like

this (   ), tapping it will take you back to the main screen of your Kindle, where you'll be presented with the Carousel (more on this in a bit) and the Home Screen (more on this in a bit, too).

Next is the Menu button. Whenever you see an icon that looks like this

(   ), tapping it will bring up context-specific options that are related to the app or section of your Kindle that you are in. Tapping it while looking at your Books, for example, will display a popup that allows you to change how your books are displayed in your HDX's bookshelf. Because this button is context-specific, what it does can change depending on what program it's in.

Next is the Back button. Whenever you see an icon that looks like this ( ) or this ( ), tapping it will take you back a step in whatever you were doing. Like the Menu button, the Back button is somewhat context specific, and it can take you "back" through things like web pages, apps that were open, sections in the settings menu that you are exploring and so forth. The key to remember is this: if you want to back up a step in whatever you're doing, try the Back button first!

Finally, the last common icon you'll use for navigation is the Search button. Whenever you see an icon that looks like this ( ), tapping it will bring up a search in whatever you happen to be looking at. Like the Menu and Back buttons, the Search button is also somewhat context specific,

Sleeping

When your HDX is in Sleep mode, it uses much less energy than normal. In Sleep mode, the screen is turned off. Your HDX comes preset to automatically enter Sleep mode after 5 minutes passes without any activity. You can also put the device into Sleep mode by pressing and releasing the power button. To exit Sleep mode and bring up the Lock Screen again, simply press and release the power button.

Notifications

The narrow bar at the very top of virtually every screen on your HDX is called the **Notification** bar. Right now, the Notification bar on my HDX looks like this:

Your Notification bar may look different depending on what apps you have running, what version of the HDX you have and other factors. In light of that fact, let's go through what the Notification bar tells us through the use of all those little icons.

Name – The name of your HDX is displayed at the far left of the Navigation Bar and can be edited in your account online as explained later in this guide book.

– A number inside a circle indicates that a certain number of notifications are pending your viewing or dismissal. Swipe down to reveal the notifications.

– These icons indicate whether your batter is full, needs to be charged or is charging. If you've chosen to display the remaining charge percentage, it will be shown to the left of the battery meter.

– If Bluetooth is enabled, a pale Bluetooth symbol will be displayed. If Bluetooth is enabled and your HDX is paired with a Bluetooth device, then the symbol will become solid.

– If this icon is present, then Quiet Time has been activated on your HDX and notifications will be silenced and hidden while it is active.

– If this symbol is present, then an app or a website is using your Wi-Fi signal to estimate your physical location.

– This lock is active when parental controls are turned on and enabled, thus restricting access to certain content.

– If this cute airplane is showing up, it means that all wireless functionality on your HDX has been disabled, so you can't connect to the internet.

– If you're mirroring your HDX's screen, this icon will be present.

– A Wi-Fi symbol that's greyed out with an X on it means that Wi-Fi is turned on and your HDX is connected to a network, but you can't access the Internet. An icon that is just greyed out means that your Wi-Fi is enabled, but you're not connected to the internet. If the icon is filled in at all, that means you're connected to a network, and how much of the icon is filled in will indicate the relative signal strength of the connection (more of the icon filled in means a better connection).

Quick Settings

The Quick Settings menu is one you'll access quite often, and as such, it's easy to access. Just swipe your finger down from the top of the display to pull open the Quick Settings menu, which might look something like this:

You'll notice that there are more than a few things going on in this screenshot, so let's take a look at all of them to see what they are.

First off, along the top of the Quick Settings menu, below the

Notifications bar, you have the Auto-Rotate lock button ( ). Tapping this will engage the auto-rotate lock, which will prevent the screen from shifting positions as you move the HDX around. Tap again to disengage this lock and allow the screen to rotate freely.

Next is the Brightness button (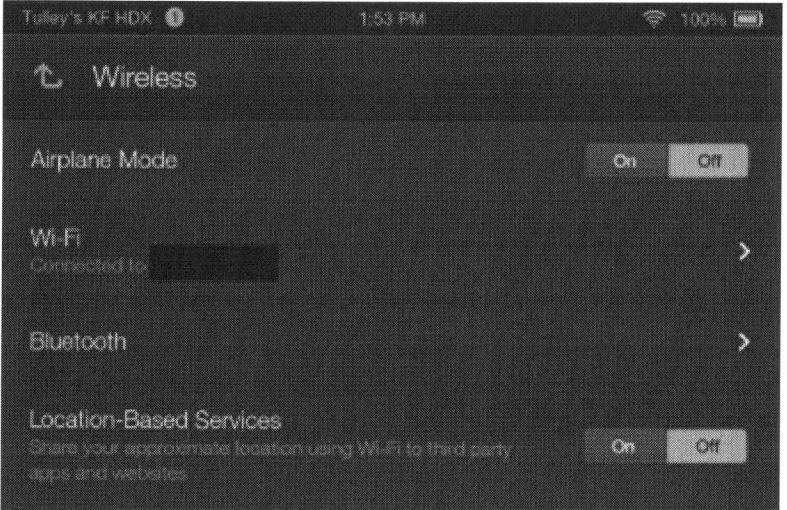). Tapping this will bring up a brightness slider, which you can slide left and right to adjust how bright you want the screen to be. Underneath the slider is an auto-brightness toggle. When turned on, the HDX will auto-adjust the brightness and disable the manual brightness slider.

Next is the Wireless button (). This opens a new menu with several options on it:

Airplane mode, when turned on, disables all wireless communications on your HDX. Tapping the Wi-Fi or Bluetooth options will take you into the wireless connectivity settings for Wi-Fi and Bluetooth, which we'll go over a bit later in this guide. Turning Location-Based Services on will allow third-party apps and websites to track your location based on your Wi-Fi signal.

Quiet time ( ), when engaged with a quick tap, will mute all notifications and alert sounds on your HDX, giving you a chance to focus on whatever you're doing.

The Mayday button ( ), which we'll go over shortly in a later section, opens the Amazon Assist section of your HDX, and brings you to within one tap of talking live with an Amazon support representative.

Finally, the Settings button ( ) opens the advanced settings of your Kindle, which we'll go over a little later in this guide.

The Mayday Button & Amazon Assist

When you tap the Mayday button ( ) in the Quick Settings pull-down menu, you'll be taken to a screen that looks something like this:

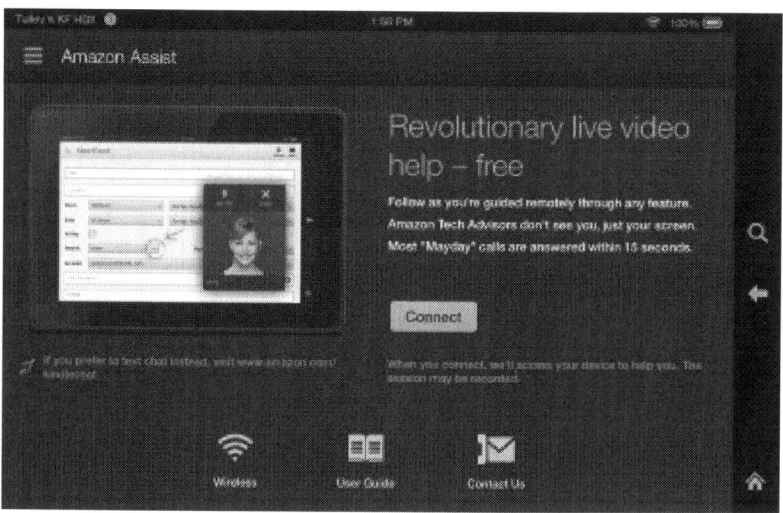

Mayday is an amazing feature that puts you on a live voice chat with a Kindle tech advisor in an average of 15 seconds or less. You'll be able to see and hear the tech advisor as they talk to you, though they won't see you. They will be able to hear you, though, and once you're connected with them, you can chat with them about your questions regarding your HDX. I tested out this feature and was connected with a very nice gentleman whose name and face I won't disclose for his own privacy, but this is what I saw when he was talking to me:

I asked him a question about the USB connection on the HDX, and he was quick to answer and seemed like he was well-trained in all things

Kindle. Whenever you have a question about your Kindle that you can't find the answer to anywhere else, go ahead and tap the Mayday button and then tap the yellow Connect button (Connect) to start chatting with a tech advisor.

If you don't think your question is that urgent, there are other options! At the bottom of the Amazon Assist screen, you'll see three sections which connect you with other help options.

The Wireless (Wireless) icon opens up a section of help texts that will guide you through troubleshooting common wireless connectivity issues.

The User Guide (User Guide) icon opens up the HDX's user guide, which contains basic information on how to use your HDX.

Finally, the Contact Us (Contact Us) icon will help you get in touch with Amazon tech support via phone or email, or allow you to send them feedback about a particular feature on your Kindle.

Charging

Your HDX should have come with a micro-USB cable and a power adapter. This power adapter looks like a small black box with a USB port and retractable prongs for inserting into a power outlet. To charge your HDX, insert the small end of the micro-USB cable into the micro-USB slot your HDX. This slot is located at the bottom edge, near the power button. Once the small end of the micro-USB cable is inserted into the HDX, insert the other end of the USB cable into the power adapter, and then plug the power adapter into a wall electrical outlet. Note that when your Kindle is charging, you'll see the battery symbol in the Notifications bar with a lightning bolt through the center, indicating that the HDX is charging.

If you plug your HDX into your computer or a 3rd party power adapter to charge it, you may see the following message appear when you turn it on:

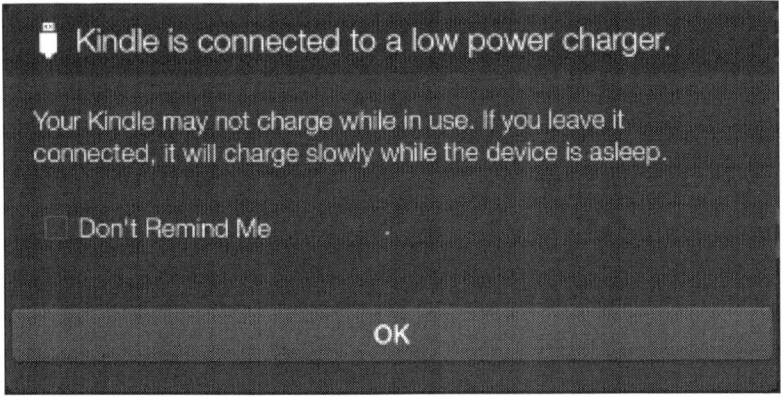

This is normal, and is merely an indication that the power provided to your HDX by your computer's USB port is insufficient to charge the HDX at a normal pace. Your HDX may not charge if you use it while it is plugged in to a low power charger, but if you press the power button or leave the device alone to put it to sleep, it will slowly charge over time.

Restart

If something goes horribly wrong and you need to restart your HDX, there's a simple way to do so. Press and hold the power button on the back of the HDX for about three seconds, or until you see the following popup appear:

Tap the **Power Off** button and wait for the HDX to turn completely off. Once it's off and the screen is black, press the power button again to turn it back on. Note that if your HDX is completely unresponsive and the power options popup doesn't appear, hold the power button for around twenty seconds to force the HDX to power off. You can then power it back on in the normal fashion.

Volume Settings

There are two ways to adjust the volume on your HDX. The first is with the physical volume buttons on the top back of the device. The second is through the on-screen slider. To change the volume in this manner, swipe down from the top of the screen to open the Quick Settings menu, then tap Settings, then Display & Sounds. Move the volume slider back and forth to adjust the volume up and down.

When something is playing audio actively (such as a video or piece of music), the app that's playing the audio will often have a volume slider built into it that will give you quick on-screen access to changing the volume without having to go through the Settings menu. Just be sure to look for the Volume icon ( ) in apps that play sound to find these built-in volume adjustments.

Headphones

While your Kindle Fire HDX has some fantastic built-in speakers, sometimes headphones are the only way to go. You can plug a pair of headphones into the 3.5mm jack at the top of the HDX, near the volume buttons. You'll still be able to adjust the volume through the buttons or the on-screen volume controls, but as long as headphones are plugged into the jack, all of the HDX's sounds will be routed through them instead of the speakers.

Screen Brightness

Screen brightness on the HDX is pretty simple. The brighter the screen, the easier it is to see, but the more energy it burns. Having the screen be brighter while the surrounding lights are also bright will make the screen easier to see, but dimming the brightness while you are in darker surroundings will make it easier to see as well. Confused? Don't worry. Controlling the brightness is very easy, and if you don't want to, you don't have to control it yourself at all.

Swipe down from the top of the screen to open the Quick Settings bar, then tap the Brightness button. This will bring up a brightness slider, which you can slide left and right to adjust how bright you want the screen to be. Underneath the slider is an auto-brightness toggle. When turned on, the HDX will auto-adjust the brightness and disable the manual brightness slider.

The Navigation Bar

Sitting below the notification bar and above the Carousel, the Navigation bar is going to be one of your most frequently-accessed sections:

Containing shortcuts to essentially all of your digital media, the navigation bar makes it easy to access apps, music, videos, photos and more, all with a tap of the finger. Let's go through each section and explain what you'll find inside of them. We'll go through some of these sections in more detail later.

– This shortcut to the search function lets you search across your Kindle, Amazon's store and the web at large.

Shop – This takes you to Amazon's shopping app, where you can shop for physical and digital products right from your HDX.

Games – Here you'll find the games you've downloaded to your HDX, the games that you purchased/downloaded that are still in the Cloud and a shortcut to shop for more games to download.

Apps – Like the Games shortcut, the Apps shortcut does the same thing, but for apps!

Books – Again, this shortcut is pretty self-explanatory, showing you both your local, cloud and Amazon store books that you can purchase.

Music – This gives you access not only to your music, but to the Kindle music player as well.

Videos – Amazon's wide selection of TV shows and movies is accessible through this shortcut, both content you have purchased/rented and content available as part of your Amazon Prime subscription. You... do have an Amazon Prime subscription, right?

Newsstand – Magazines are something I never bother to look at on my Kindle, but if you're interested in purchasing magazines or magazine subscriptions, here's where you'll find them!

Audiobooks – Audiobooks are a big part of the Kindle reading experience since so many novels these days have professionally narrated audiobooks that go along with them (there's more on this later in the guide book). If you've purchased any audiobooks, here's where you'll find them.

Web – This one's simple: just a shortcut to the Silk web browser!

Photos – Photos that you've uploaded to your HDX or taken with the built-in camera (as well as screenshots you may have taken) are stored here.

Docs – Any documents you upload to the Documents folder on your Kindle through your computer or other means will be accessible through this shortcut.

Offers – Finally, if you have Special Offers enabled, you can see a list of all of the offers under this shortcut. If you've turned off Special Offers (or if you don't have an HDX with Special Offers on it to begin with), this shortcut won't be present.

The Carousel

The Carousel is the central part of your HDX's user interface, and you'll be using it a lot. Your most recently used apps, books, movies and more are shown here in a series of icons that you can zip through by swiping to the left or right.

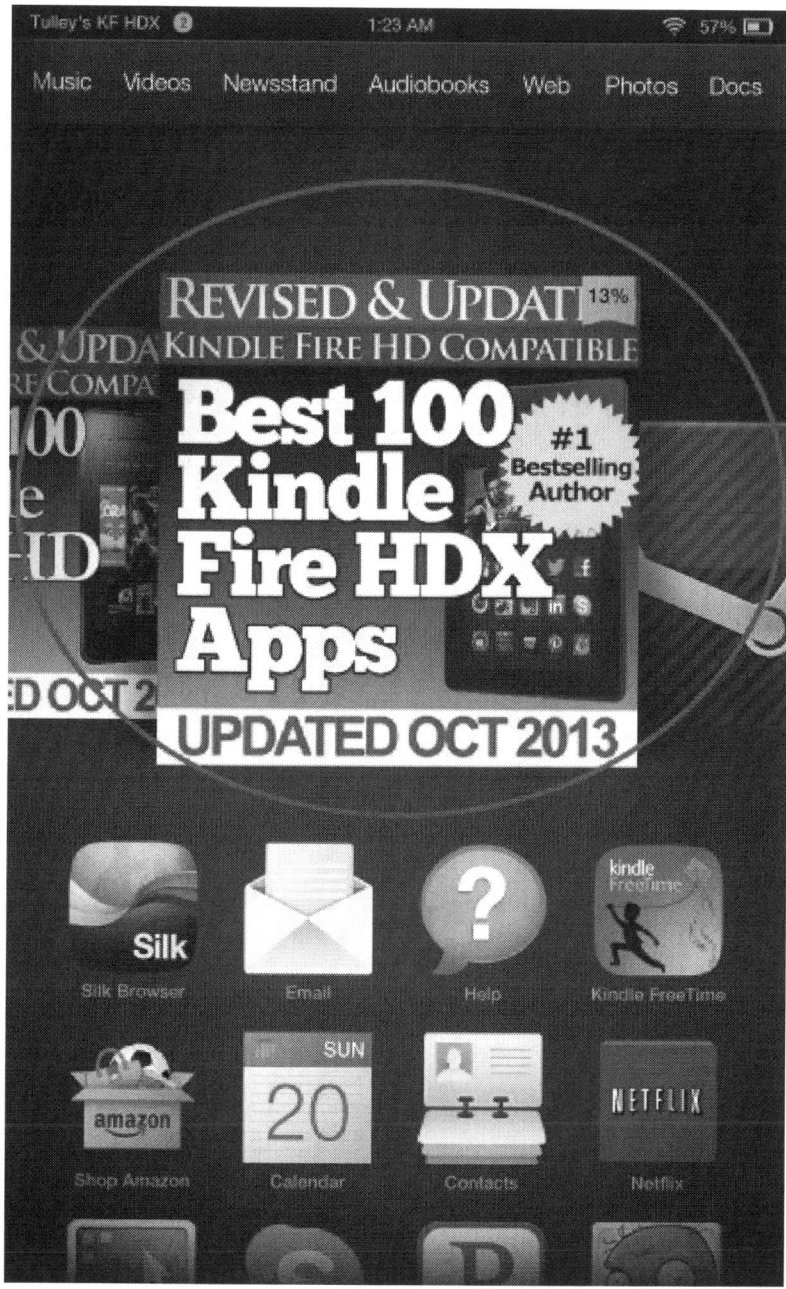

Tap on an item in the Carousel to open it, or, if you wish to remove it, press and hold on the item until the following popup appears:

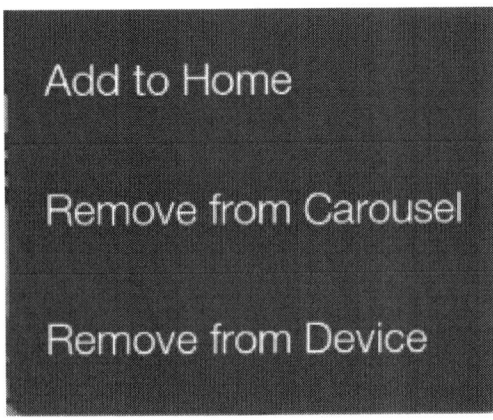

Tap **Remove from Carousel** to remove the item from the Carousel. Note that when you choose this option, the item will merely vanish from the Carousel, but it will still be on your device. To remove an item from your device, tap the **Remove from Device** option. Items that you purchase from Amazon will still remain in your Cloud storage, but you will have to re-download them to access them again. Items that you stored locally on your HDX will be deleted when you use this option.

Turning On/Off Recommendations

You may have noticed that a small row of icons appears under the Carousel for items that you purchased, downloaded or viewed from Amazon:

This list of icons is a series of recommendations which are really just advertisements trying to get you to purchase more stuff from Amazon.

If you want to free up the clutter that the recommendations section causes, swipe down from the top of the screen to expose the Quick Settings menu, tap Settings, tap Applications, then tap Home Screen. You should see a menu like this appear:

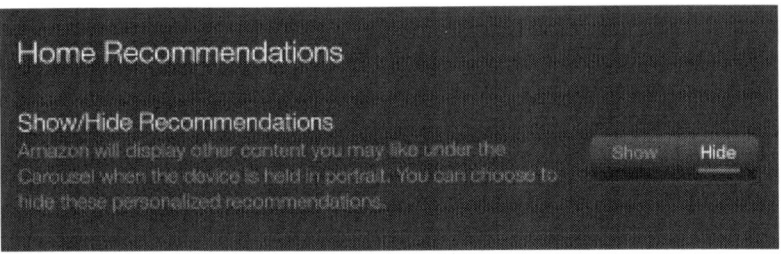

Tap the Hide option to prevent recommendations from being displayed on your HDX's home screen. Note that you can also turn this option back on if you really want to. Removing the recommendations will increase the space for your Home Screen under the Carousel, which we'll look at next.

The Home Screen

What Amazon calls the Home Screen I call the App Drawer, but the principle is the same regardless of what name you call it. This is where you can store your most frequently used apps, music, games and other digital content for quick access:

To add an app, piece of music or other piece of digital media to the
Home Screen, tap and hold on the item until a popup like this appears:

Select the Add to Home option to add it to your Home Screen. Note that for some media (such as TV shows, for example), the item will need to be in your local library or your Carousel for this popup to appear. Trying to tap and hold to make the popup appear when you're browsing the Book or Videos stores, for example, won't work.

Note that in this guide book and in the official Amazon references, both the "App Drawer" and the main screen containing the Carousel (the screen you get to when you tap the Home button) are referred to as the "Home screen." In this guide book, I've made an effort to distinguish the two by using the phrase "Home Screen" when referring to what I call the "App Drawer" and using the phrase "Home screen" to refer to the general "home page" of the HDX.

The Options Bar

On any screen except the Home/Carousel screen, you should be able to see the Options Bar at the bottom of the screen. If you don't see it, just tap the center of the screen and it should appear. A variety of icons can appear on the Options bar, including a few of the ones we talked about earlier (Home, Back, Menu and Search). The icon that we didn't talk about that can appear in the Options bar only appears occasionally, and looks like this:

Tapping this while the on-screen keyboard is open will cause the keyboard to disappear.

The other awesome feature about the Options Bar is that swiping from the edge of the screen where the options bar is located towards the center of the screen will make a miniature Carousel appear, where you can swipe up/down or left/right (depending on how you are holding your HDX) to browse through the items in the Carousel:

Tap on an icon in this "mini-Carousel" to switch directly to that item without having to return to the Home screen first.

Disabling Special Offers

Each of the Kindle HDX models comes with the option to purchase it at a reduced cost at the expense of having "Special Offers" turned on. What are Special Offers? Well, if you have an HDX with Special Offers, you see them every time you wake your device up from sleep mode and see an advertisement on the Lock screen. These offers are fairly unobtrusive, but they can be an eyesore if you like a clean, elegant interface.

Fortunately, it's pretty easy to get rid of Special Offers. To do so, log in to your Amazon account on your computer and open the Your Account section. Scroll down and select the Manage Your Kindle option, entering your password again if requested. Next, select Manage Your Devices and then select your Kindle HDX from the list of devices.

Click the Edit link next to line that says "Special Offers: Subscribed" and you'll be given a cost to disable Special Offers. At the moment, this cost is $15, and if you click the "Unsubscribe now with 1-Click" button, Special Offers will be immediately disabled on your HDX. This setting will take effect the next time it syncs up and the Lock screen pulls up, though, so don't worry if they don't instantly disappear, because they will very soon.

Favoriting Items

If you had a Kindle Fire HD, you might have remembered the Favorites button, and how you could long-press on digital items to add them to your favorites. The Favorites section is gone now, and is instead replaced with something similar to the original Kindle Fire, the Home Screen (though I like to refer to it as the "App Drawer"). Whenever you long tap on an item and select the option to add it to "Home," that causes the item to be added to your Home Screen, which sits below the Carousel. For more details on the Home Screen, turn back a few pages in this guide book.

The Navigation Panel

When you're browsing through pretty much any library, such as your Books (through the Books shortcut in the Navigation Bar), if you swipe from left to right starting at the far left edge of the screen, the Navigation Panel will appear. You can also access this panel by tapping

this ( ) button, located in the upper left corner of your content libraries and some apps.

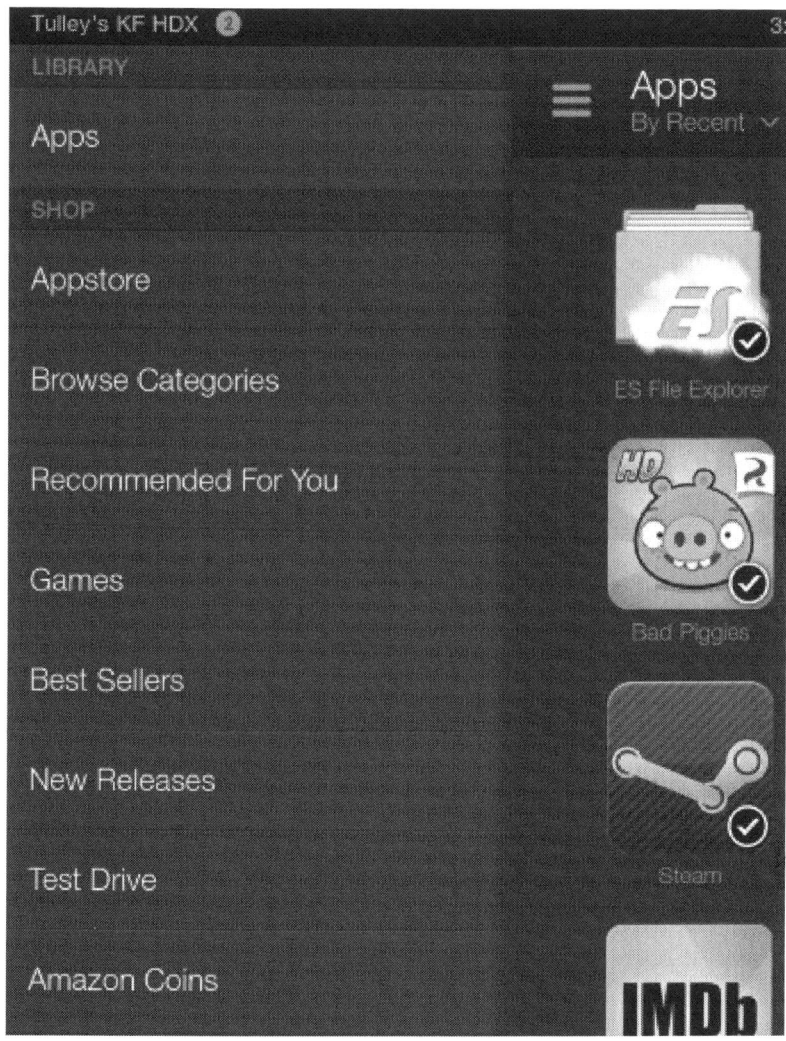

The Navigation panel's purpose is to give you quick access to relevant content. This content might be from your content library or from Amazon's shop, but whatever the case may be, the Navigation Panel will get you there.

When you're reading a book (like this one!), you can swipe from left to right to reveal the navigation panel, but only after tapping the center of the screen first. Alternatively, just tap the center of the screen, then tap the nav panel icon in the upper left-hand corner to open the Navigation Panel.

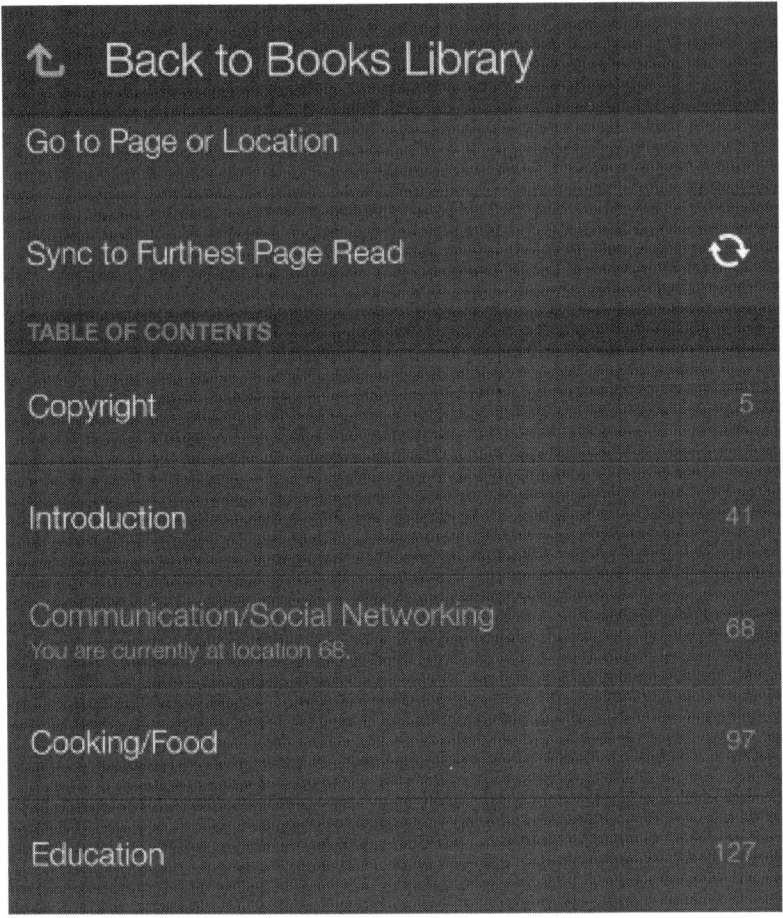

For books, the Navigation Panel primarily serves as a way to quickly jump around books by letting you browse through the Table of Contents or type in pages/locations in a book you want to go to. This "Go To" option is a bit wonky at the moment, and doesn't always show the Table of Contents for books properly, even if they're properly formatted.

Search

Whether you access the HDX's search function through the Options Bar, the Navigation Bar or through another location, searching through your HDX's content is a snap. Search on the HDX does more than that, though. You can search through Amazon's shops for apps, books, music, movies and even do a general web search, all from the same search box.

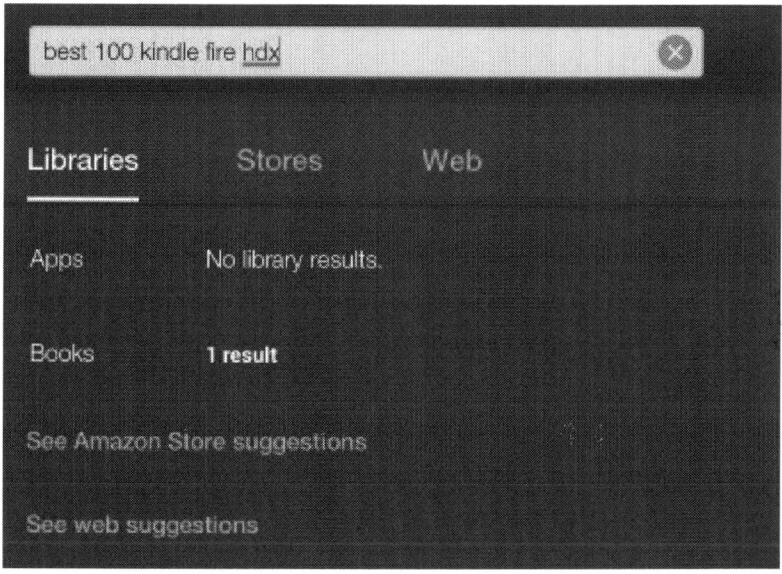

To get started, tap the Search icon (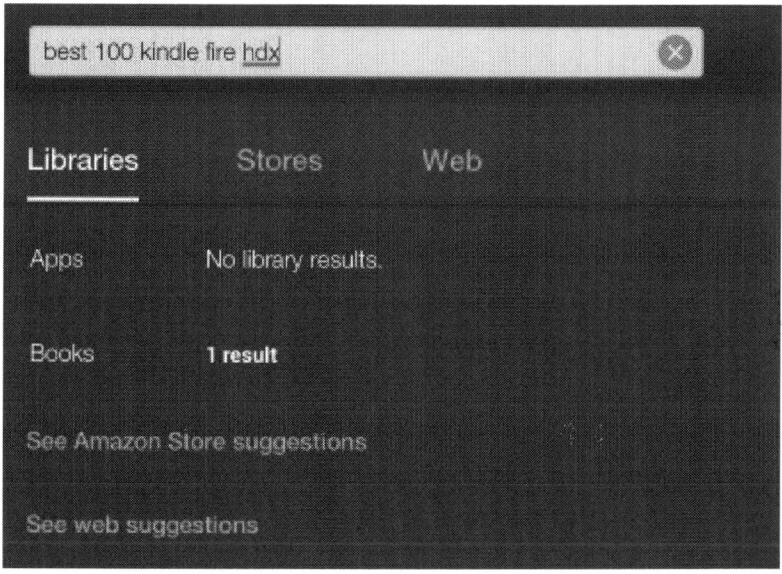) anywhere on your HDX and then type in your search term(s). In this example below, I'm going to search for my Best 100 Kindle Fire HDX Apps book.

As you can see, there are three different search results tabs: Libraries, Stores and Web. In the Libraries tab, there's one result for my search term under Books, which is correct because I added my apps book to my HDX's local library. Tapping on the Stores tab brings up results for the search term in Amazon's stores while tapping the Web tab will bring up search results for the search term by performing a web search in the Silk browser.

Note that the search results have to be tapped on to see the full results. For example, if I tap on the result in the Web tab, a search is performed on Google in the Silk browser for that search term.

Let's go through one more quick example to show how well this works. I'll enter the search term (without quotes) of "mass effect" in the search box, then tap on the Stores tab to see these results:

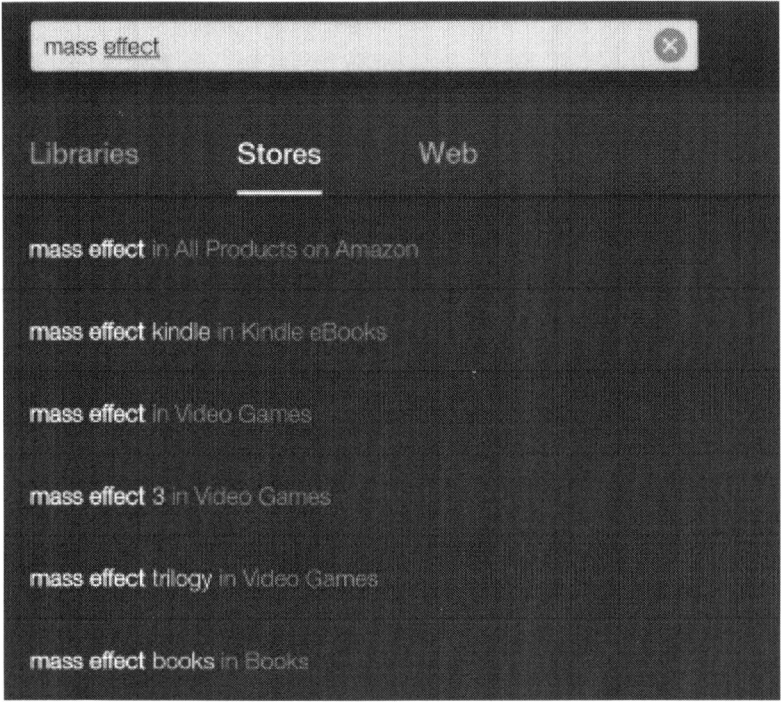

In the results, I can see that I have options to perform a search for this term in the Kindle store, on Amazon in general, in the Video Games category and other locations. I also see more search term suggestions, such as "mass effect trilogy" and "mass effect books" which I can tap on. Swiping up in the search results list reveals more search suggestions, all of which I can tap on to view results for that search term in the specified location.

Likewise, if I switch to the Web tab for the same search result, I see these results:

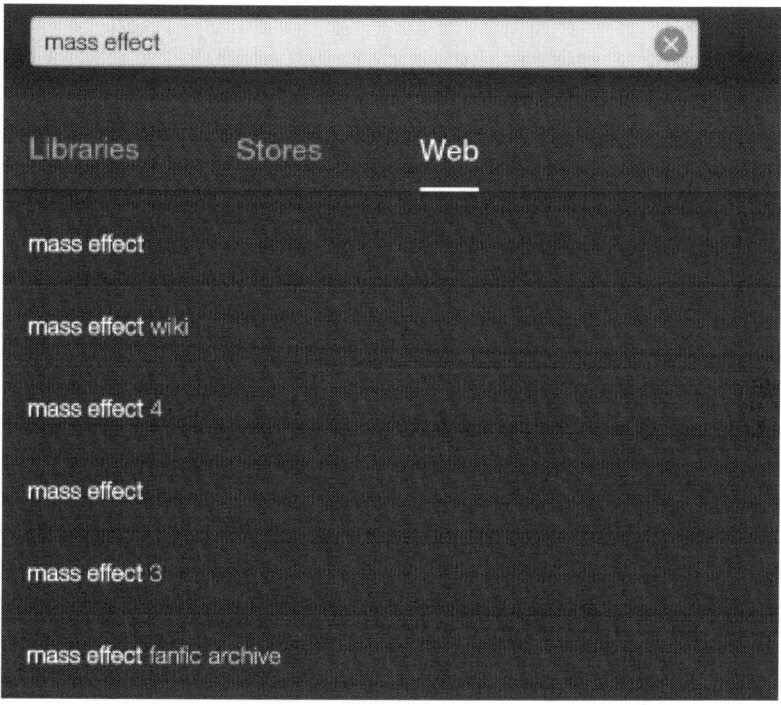

Tapping on any one of these search results will open the web browser and perform an automatic search in my default search engine for the search term.

So, not only is the Search function handy for looking through your local library of books, music, videos and other digital items, but it's a quick way to perform searches on Amazon's stores and on the web as well.

Connecting to Your Kindle Fire HDX

Wi-Fi Connections

Wi-Fi is the way your HDX connects to the Internet. Without Wi-Fi, you can't browse Amazon's shops, download files, surf the web or do anything except access local content on your HDX. When you first set up your HDX in the beginning section of this guide book, we covered how to initially join a Wi-Fi network, but now let's go through how to do that (and manage your Wi-Fi connections as a whole) again, as the process is slightly different.

Swipe down from the top of the screen to reveal the Quick Settings bar, then tap the Wireless button. Tap the Wi-Fi button (which might say "Connected to <network name>" if you're connected to Wi-Fi already) to get to a screen that looks like this:

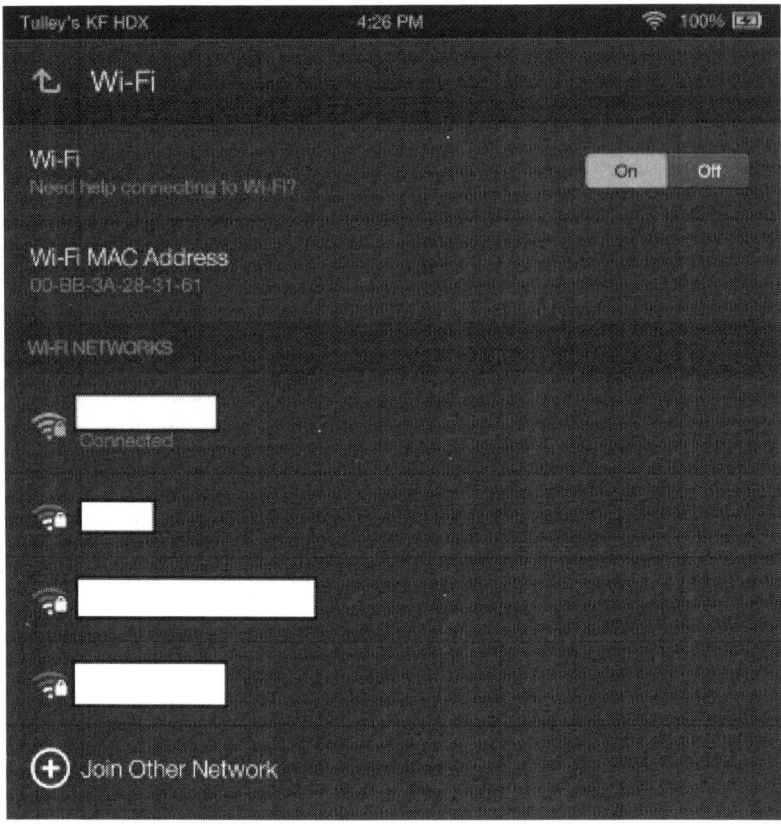

From here, you can turn Wi-Fi on or off, view your MAC Address (unneeded for anything except advanced routing issues), view what wireless network you're connected to (I've blanked out my network name for security purposes) and connect to another network.

From here, you have two choices to connect to a network. You can either tap the name of the network to join it, or you can tap the Join Other Network button. Either way, you'll see a popup like this:

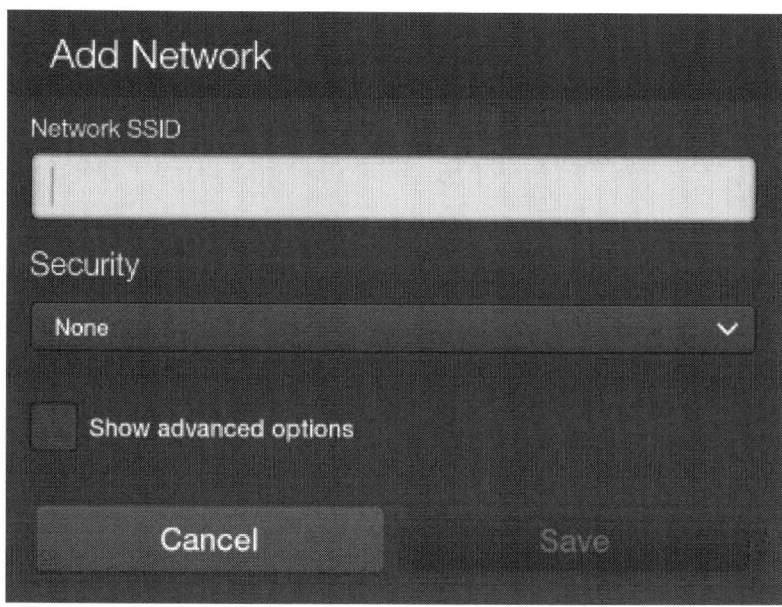

Type in the name of the network (if required) as well as the security information required to access the network. Once done, tap the Save button. Your HDX will attempt to access the network and, if the information you entered was correct, will connect to the network and you'll be ready to go!

If you want your HDX to no longer automatically connect to a network, tap and hold on the network name until a popup appears and then tap Forget Network. If you want to view advanced information about the network, tap Advanced Settings instead. From the next popup that appears, you can change the password your HDX uses for the network, view your HDX's assigned IP address, set up proxy server settings and view other advanced information about the network and your connection to it.

Social Media Connections

Your HDX comes with the built-in ability to share notes with your Facebook and Twitter friends and followers. By linking your HDX with your Facebook and Twitter accounts, you'll have access to do this anytime you're online.

Swipe down from the top to open the Quick Settings menu, then tap Settings, then tap My Account, then tap Social Network Accounts.

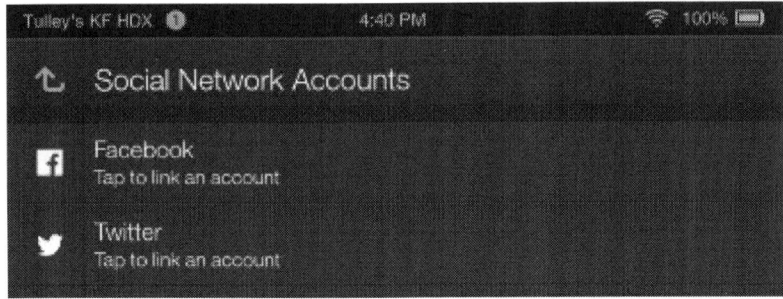

From here, tap on either the Facebook or Twitter option and type in your username and password, then tap Connect to link those accounts with your HDX.

Bluetooth

Bluetooth is baked in to your Kindle Fire HDX, making it easy for you to connect Bluetooth keyboards, headphones and whatever other devices you fancy. Let's go through an example of connecting a Bluetooth keyboard to the HDX, starting from the top.

First things first: Swipe down to open the Quick Settings menu, then tap the Wireless button, then tap the Bluetooth section. Make sure Bluetooth is turned on, then tap Pair a Bluetooth Device.

Tap Scan and then tap on the device that you want to pair with your HDX. Make sure the device is turned on and is in discoverable mode, if applicable.

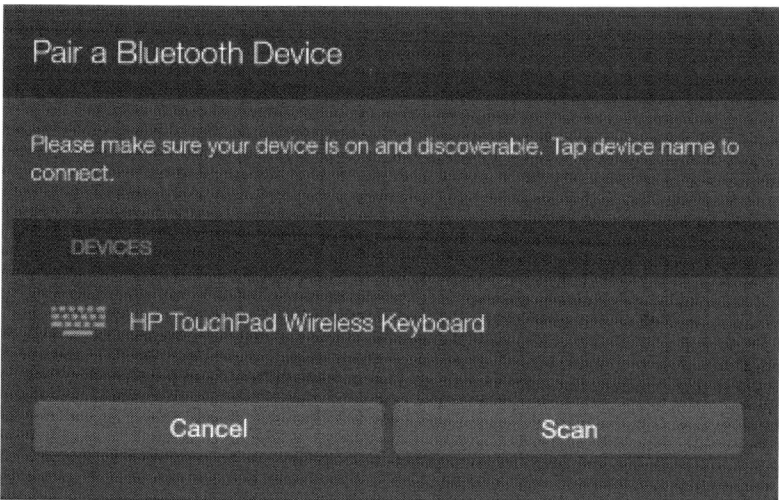

Depending on the device, you may have to enter a code on the device to confirm the pairing. Once the confirmation is complete, the device will be paired and linked to your HDX so that you can use it freely.

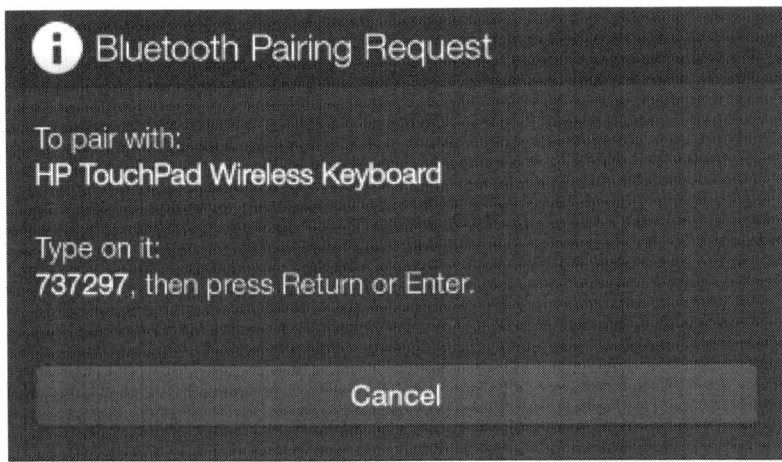

Note that having Bluetooth turned on will cause your HDX's battery to drain faster, so it's a good idea to turn it off unless you're actively using a paired Bluetooth device.

To remove a Bluetooth device from your HDX's stored device list, tap and hold on the device name in the Bluetooth section and then tap the Forget option in the popup that appears.

Data Transfers & Digital Content

USB Data Transfer

Transferring data to your HDX is fast and easy with a USB connection. Once you've connected your HDX to your computer, the HDX appears as a media device that you can open and browse with a file browser. If you want to transfer documents (books, .PDF documents, .DOC/.DOCX documents, etc) to your HDX, just drag and drop them into the Documents folder on the HDX.

To access these documents once you've transferred them to your HDX, tap the Docs button in the Navigation Bar above the Carousel on the Home screen and make sure that On Device is selected.

You'll notice that if you add a document to your library, it will automatically appear in the Carousel on your Home screen, as well as be accessible through the Docs button on the Navigation Bar. Furthermore, you'll notice that there are some buttons/icons for helping you add more documents to your library (swipe from the left or tap the Navigation Panel icon in the upper left corner and then tap Add Docs to Your Library if you don't see these icons or buttons):

Tap on any of these icons to read instructions for how to add documents to your library through email, cloud sync, article clipping (all of which we'll cover next) and through USB.

Email Data Transfer

From inside the Docs library, swipe from the left to open the Navigation Panel and then tap Add Docs to your Library. Tap Email Docs to your Kindle and your private @kindle.com email address will appear. Whenever you send documents to this email address as attachments, Amazon will convert them and upload them to your device. The downside to this approach is that you may be charged for the conversion and upload depending on your market and the size of the documents.

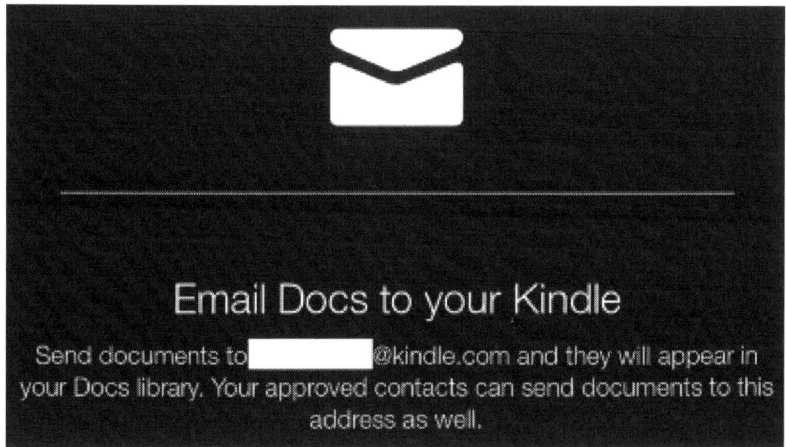

Amazon Cloud Drive Sync

From inside the Docs library, swipe from the left to open the Navigation Panel and then tap Sync with Cloud Drive. Tap the Email me install links button and Amazon will send an email to your Amazon account email address with links to download and install Cloud Drive sharing software. Once you install this software and transfer documents into it as instructed, said documents will appear in the Cloud section of your Docs library.

Clipping Articles

From inside the Docs library, swipe from the left to open the Navigation Panel and then tap Clip articles from the web. Tap the Email me install links button and Amazon will send an email to your Amazon account email address with links to download and install Send-to-Kindle software for Firefox and Chrome browsers. Once installed, this software will allow you to save web content as snippets that are automatically transferred to your HDX for you to read at your leisure.

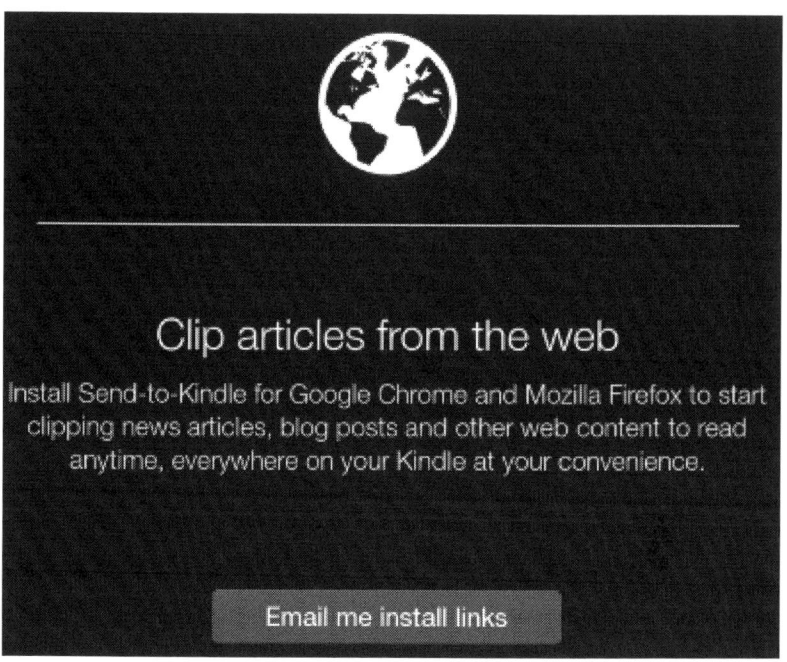

Transferring Other Digital Content

As you may have guessed by now, you can also transfer other digital content (specifically music and movies) from your computer to your HDX that the HDX can then natively play. Music and Video folders exist on the Kindle just like the Documents folder does, and you should copy music and videos from your computer via a USB connection to their respective folders on the Kindle, using a file browser just like in the example above of for performing document file transfers via USB.

One thing to note here is that not all file types and encodings are natively supported by the HDX. I can confirm that MP3 music files play properly, as do certain AVI encodings, but beyond that there is no comprehensive list of which file codecs are supported as of yet.

Finally—and this is going to seem counter-intuitive—when you want to listen to music you've transferred via USB, you go to the Music section on the Navigation Bar, then select On Device. For videos, however, you actually have to go to the Photos section of the Navigation bar, and your video that you uploaded will be there. Why it was done this way, I'm not sure, but your USB transferred videos will appear under the Photos section of the Navigation Bar, not under the Videos section.

Using the HDX Keyboard

Keyboard Basics

This is the on-screen keyboard for the Kindle Fire HDX:

You'll notice that there's a symbol key () that, when tapped, will reveal a keyboard in this layout:

Tapping the ABC key () will take you back to letter input, while

tapping the ~\< key ( ) will take you to more advanced symbols you can input:

Tapping and holding on keys will let you access their secondary key functions, which are displayed in the upper and lower right corners of the keys. For example, pressing and holding the "q" key will let you type "1" instead (without switching to the symbols keyboard) and pressing and holding the spacebar will let you choose what keyboard language to use.

To change your keyboard settings, press and hold the spacebar, then tap Keyboard Settings. On the page that appears (which we'll cover in the Advanced Settings section of this guide book), you can change all sorts of settings for your HDX's keyboard.

Press and hold the ABCKEY or ?123KEY key until a small popup appears, then release to gain access to editing functions. These include cut ( ), copy ( ), paste ( ) and select all (

). The select all key will select all text in the area that you're viewing. If you wish to select a small amount of text to cut, copy or paste, tap and hold on a word in the text until two draggable pointers appear:

Drag these pointers around in the text until the text you want is highlighted, then choose what you want to do with the selection from the small popup that appears nearby:

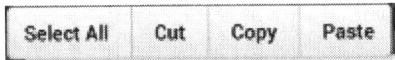

To make the keyboard disappear, tap the appropriate button ( ) on the Options Bar below the keyboard.

Tap Input

Tap input in the most basic and straightforward input on the HDX keyboard. Just think of it like a regular keyboard, except it's on-screen instead of a separate physical device. Using portrait mode and both hands, you can cover both sides of the keyboard with your thumbs for inputting text, or you can hold the device with one hand and input with the other, or some other arrangement that you prefer better.

Swype Input

The Kindle Fire HDX's keyboard also features an advanced input method called Swype. How this works is, instead of tapping out each letter individually, you put your finger down on the first letter of the word and then quickly drag your finger across the keyboard, "swyping" your finger between the letters of that word. The awesome thing about this type of input is that you don't have to be precise about where you swipe your finger; the Swype software interprets everything and makes extremely accurate judgments about what words you want to type out. For example, if I wanted to type the word "amazon" with Swype, I'd move my finger in the following pattern on the keyboard:

As you swipe your finger around, an orange line follows, showing you where you've been.

Once you reach the last letter of the word, lift your finger and the word that Swype thinks you meant will be entered in. If that wasn't the word you meant, though, a series of other similar suggestions will be displayed above the keyboard in the suggested words section above the keyboard.

You don't need to pause in between Swyped words to insert spaces with the spacebar, as spaces are automatically inserted for you when appropriate. Punctuation such as commas and periods will not be automatically inserted, though, so be sure to put those in yourself.

Remember: you don't have to be accurate when Swyping! It's the pattern that matters, so after you get used to how it works, you can Swype out words much faster than you can tap them out, and retain even greater accuracy due to Swype's advanced processing algorithms.

The Kindle Fire HDX Browser

Silk Browser Basics

Amazon's Silk browser is baked into the HDX's operating system and is the only official web browser available (unless you side load a different one, which we'll talk about a little later in this guide).

To open Silk, tap the Web button on the Navigation Bar on the Home screen, and you'll see a window like this appear:

This screen will appear the first time you start the browser, or when you open a new tab before typing in a URL. Whenever you're viewing a web page and you close the browser, you'll be shown your last viewed page when you open it back up.

The basic controls for the Silk browser are as follows:

– Type in URLs or search terms in the Address Bar, then tap Go on the keyboard to visit the site or perform the search.

– Tap this button to open a new tab (maximum of 10 at any one time). Close an open tab by tapping the **x** on the right side of the tab title. If you open more than a few tabs, you can browse between them by swiping left or right across the tabs and then tap on the tab you want to view. You can also tap and hold on a tab to bring up a menu that will let you either close the tab you were selecting, close all the other tabs that are open except for the one that you selected or close all of the tabs that are open.

– Tap this to automatically jump to the Address Bar to perform a search or type in a URL.

– Tap this to go back to the previous page.

– Tap this to go forward (useful if you've been using the back button above).

– Tap this to make the web page content fill the entire screen, hiding the Options and Address bars. You can exit full screen mode by swiping or tapping on the handle (HANDLEICON) icon.

– Our old friend, the menu icon, has some relevant operations for use in the Silk browser. When you tap it, you can choose to Share Page (through email, Facebook, Twitter, etc), Add/Edit Bookmark (add a bookmark or edit an existing one for the page you're viewing), Find in Page (perform a search on the content in the web page you're viewing) or Request Another View (choose to view either a Mobile, Desktop or Automatic version of the web page; Automatic is recommended).

Advanced Silk Settings

To access the advanced settings for the Silk Browser, swipe left to right from the left edge of the screen or tap the Navigation Panel icon. Once the Navigation Panel is open, tap the Settings button.

On this page, you'll find all sorts of settings that you can tweak to your heart's content. Let's go through them one by one. Remember, you can change the options by either unchecking or checking the box next to the option, or by tapping on the option name to open the settings selections.

Search Engine – This allows you to choose between Bing, Yahoo or Google as your default search engine provider for the browser.
Block Pop-Up Windows – Pop-ups are annoying, but silk can block them if you wish! If you want the browser to ask you each time it detects a pop-up whether or not you want to block it, choose the Ask option. If you want it to allow all pop-ups, choose the Always option. If you want to never allow pop-ups, choose the Never option.
Accelerate Page Loading – Silk has the unique ability to draw on Amazon's Cloud server system to make web pages load faster for you.

This comes at the expense of having your data re-routed through Amazon's servers, though, so there is some benefit to approaching this option with caution.

Optional Encryption – If you choose to use the Cloud system to accelerate page loading, you can tap this option to have your data encrypted as it passes through Amazon's servers. Unfortunately, choosing this option can cause the speed advantages to evaporate, which leaves you back at square one.

Enable Instant Page Loads – This option, when enabled, will pre-load links on a webpage in the background that you are likely to visit, so that if you open one, the page loads instantly on your browser. If this option is selected and a pre-loaded page is loaded up, a small lightning bolt will appear on the right side of the Address Bar to let you know why the page load was so fast.

Clear History / Clear Cache / Clear All Cookie Data / Clear Passwords / Clear Form Data – These options let you clear out your browser history, cookies that have been set by websites, the cache of web pages you've visited, any saved passwords you may have entered and any saved form data you entered. You can also choose to clear this information from individual websites by selecting the Individual Website Data option and choosing the website from the list that you want to clear the information on.

Accept Cookies – Enabling this option allows websites to save cookies to the browser, which can track and keep track of you and your information.

Enable Location – If a website wants to use your location to serve up personal region-specific information to you, you can enable the use of your location by checking this option. Each new request will be shown in a pop-up which you can confirm or deny, and you can clear all location access requests with the Clear Location Access option.

Load Images – Enable or disable the loading of images in websites.

Enable Javascript – Enable or disable the loading of Javascript on websites.

Show Security Warnings – Enable or disable pop-up warnings of issues with websites' security certificates.

Prompt for Experimental Streaming Viewer – Enable or disable the experimental streaming viewer, which will detect Flash content and run it in the browser if you choose to do so.

Reset All Settings to Default – Changes all Silk Browser settings back to their factory default settings.

Buying & Reading Books

Purchasing Books

From the Home screen, tap the Books button in the Navigation Bar, then tap the Store button in the upper right-hand corner to view the Amazon Kindle bookstore.

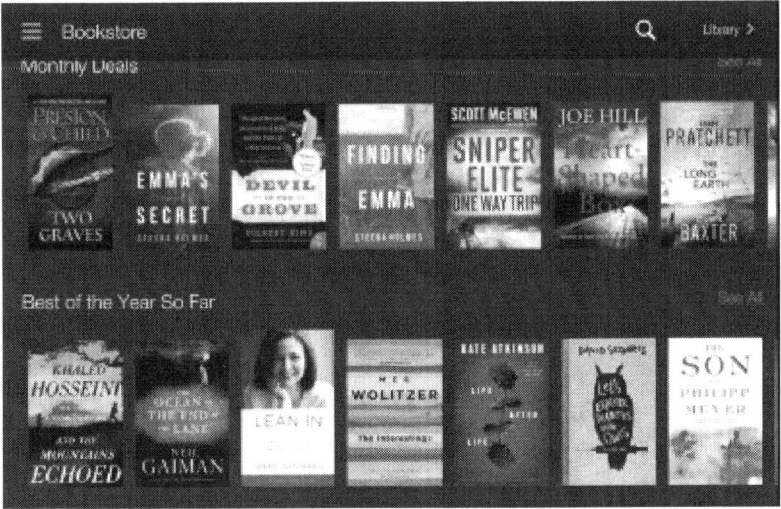

From here, you can do a few things. If you've purchased books from Amazon before, a list of recommendations will appear, as well as a rotating list of new, popular and bestselling books. By swiping up and down the screen, you can explore deeper into other genres and categories.

You can also swipe from the left edge or tap the Navigation Panel button in the upper left corner to open the Navigation Panel.

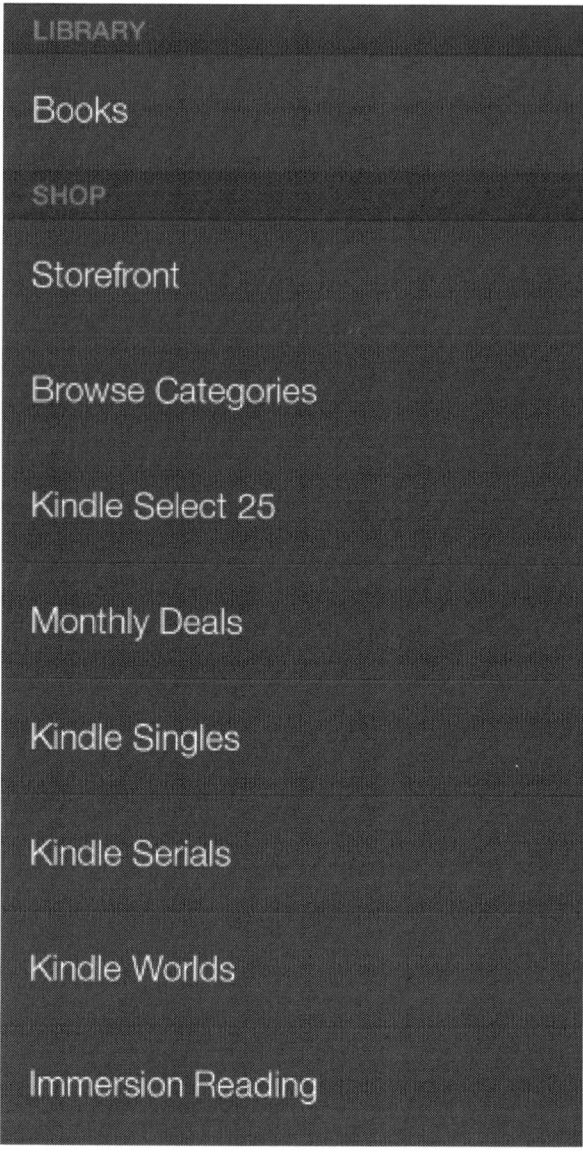

Doing so gives you fine-grained access to various book categories, any of which you can tap on to view. From a specific category, you can tap the button the right of the Navigation Panel button to view sorting options, so that you can sort the displayed books by popularity, rank and so on. You'll also be able to filter them by categories and ratings using the Categories and Filter options.

When you're ready to purchase a book, just tap the Buy button. If you're purchasing a magazine or newspaper subscription, tap the Subscribe now button instead. For books, you can also try it out for free by tapping the Download Sample button, which will let you read a small portion before giving you the option to purchase the rest.

If you have an Amazon Prime account, you can borrow one free book per month from books that are enrolled in the KDP Select program. You can identify these books by the "Prime" badge under their titles and on their details page.

To download a free Prime book, just tap the Borrow for Free button on the purchase page, and you'll be able to read the book for as long as you want, or until you borrow a different book instead.

All books, magazines and newspapers that you purchase or subscribe to are automatically downloaded to your Kindle Fire HDX, and are available under their respective sections in the Navigation Bar. For example, to view a purchased and downloaded book, tap Books in the Navigation Bar, then tap On Device, then tap the book that you want to view. Sort the books in your library with the sort options to the right of the Navigation Panel button in the upper left corner. Sort options include by author, recent and title.

If you delete a purchased book from your HDX, it still exists in the cloud, and can be re-downloaded at any time by going to your Books from the Navigation Bar, then tapping the Cloud option, then tapping the book you want to re-download.

Books, magazines and newspapers that you recently purchased or viewed are displayed in your Carousel, and can be removed from the Carousel by tapping and holding on them and then choosing the Remove from Carousel option. To remove a purchased book from your book library, tap and hold on the title and then select the Remove from Device option. These instructions apply equally for magazines and newspapers as well.

Reading Books

Once you've opened a book, you'll probably want to read it, right? No worries there! Reading a book on the HDX is simple. To start with, you can make the Navigation, Options and Progress bars at the top, right and bottom (respectively) portions of the screen disappear and reappear by tapping the center of the screen.

The sheer number of apps available for the Kindle Fire HD and HDX family of devices is mind-boggling. There are thousands upon thousands of apps for doing all sorts of different tasks. With so many apps to choose from, it can be very difficult to figure out what apps you should download (either for free, or ones that you pay for) without spending hours researching, reading reviews and testing apps.

That's where I come in! I've invested over 100 hours (and counting!) into combing through hundreds of apps in the Amazon app store to find the very best apps in several different categories. I've done this by looking at the popularity of the apps along with user comments and star ratings. I've also tested these apps on my Kindle Fire and use the majority of them on a regular basis, too.

Unlike most other 'top apps' books available today, I don't just look at the apps that are in the *Top* list in the app store. Anyone can do that (and many do!). I dig down deep into the categories to look for the hidden gems, too, so that you can be sure you're getting your money's worth when you buy this book.

Highlight sections of the book by tapping and holding on a word, then dragging the hash marks that appear to encompass the area you want to highlight. You can then choose a color to highlight, make a note about the passage you highlighted, share the highlighted passage with your social media friends/followers (requires that you have already set up Facebook/Twitter), search for the highlighted section in the book, on Wikipedia or on the web, as well as translate the section using the Bing translator.

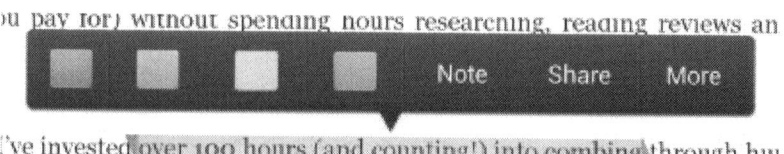

To change the font size, type and spacing, tap the Font button

Aa

( ). To set a bookmark at a particular place in the book or to edit

bookmarks you've already made, tap the Bookmarks button (Bookmarks).

Tap the Share button (Share) to share a quick thought about what you're reading with your social media followers/friends, or tap the

Notes button (Notes) to view the notes you've made on the book you're reading. Finally, if the book you're reading has been out enough for it to have been X-Ray indexed, you can tap the X-Ray button (

X-Ray) to learn more about the book's characters, story and more – Amazon touts the X-Ray feature as a way to look at the structure of a book.

Flip between pages in a book by either swiping to the right or left, or by tapping on the right or left edges of the book pages.

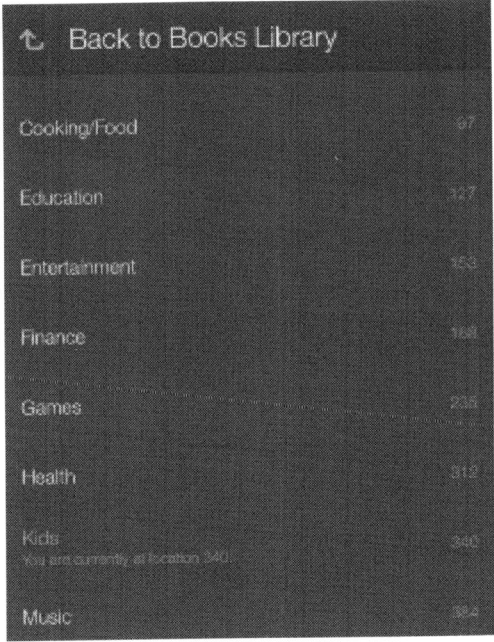

Open the Navigation Panel by tapping the button in the upper left corner of the menu or by swiping from the far left edge to reveal the Table of Contents of the book, as well as a way to type in the section in the book you want to immediately jump to.

Whispersync

Whispersync is an Amazon service that automatically synchronizes your books across all of your devices and Kindle reading apps and keeps your book progress consistent across your devices, all without you having to do anything. That means that you can start reading a book on your HDX and when you switch to read the same book on the Kindle app on your iPhone, when you open the book, it'll automatically open at the exact place where you left off on your HDX.

Using Apps

Purchasing Apps

To download free or non-free apps, you'll need to open the Apps section of the Navigation Bar on the Home screen. From here, tap on the Store button in the upper right corner and you'll be presented with the Amazon Appstore.

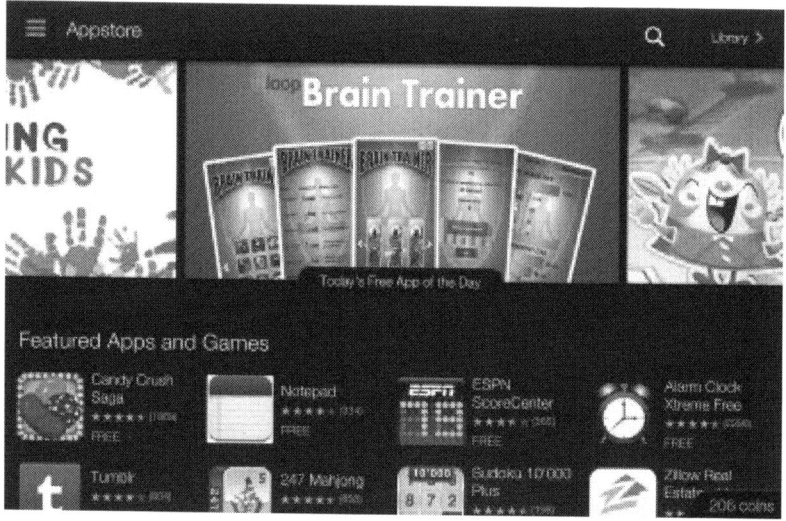

Like the bookstore, the appstore functions on the same principles. If you've purchased books from Amazon before, a list of related app recommendations will appear, as well as a rotating list of new, popular and bestselling apps. By swiping up and down the screen, you can explore deeper into other genres and categories.

You can also swipe from the left edge or tap the Navigation Panel button in the upper left corner to open the Navigation Panel.

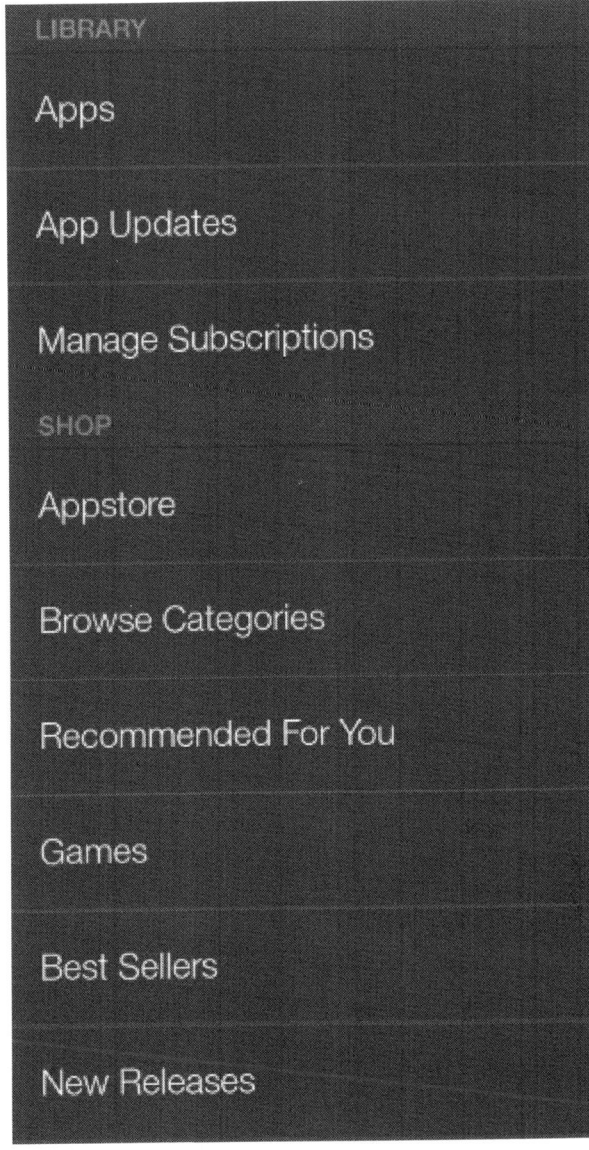

Doing so gives you fine-grained access to various app categories, any of which you can tap on to view. From a specific category, you can tap the button the right of the Navigation Panel button to view sorting options, so that you can sort the displayed books by popularity, rank and so on. You'll also be able to filter them by categories and ratings using the Categories and Filter options.

When you're ready to purchase an app, just tap the Buy or Free button, depending on whether the app requires an up-front payment or not. Most free apps contain either ads or in-app purchases, which let you purchase premium content for a fee (usually no more than a few dollars). Some paid apps will let you take them on a demo run by tapping the indicated demo button.

In addition to paying for apps with cash, you can also choose to pay for them with "coins." At the current exchange rate, one amazon coin equals one real-world penny. Buying large quantities of coins from Amazon will get you a slight discount (up to 10%), but you can't get a refund on the coins, so it's up to whether or not you want to commit the cash to Amazon or not. To purchase coins, tap on a buy button whose price looks something like this:

$6.99 or 699 coins

Tap the Buy More link to be taken to a page where you can purchase coins that you can use to buy apps with. (Only apps can be purchased with coins; not books or other digital content at this time.)

All apps that you purchase or "buy" for free are automatically downloaded to your Kindle Fire HDX, and are available under the Apps section in the Navigation Bar. To view a purchased and downloaded app, tap Apps in the Navigation Bar, then tap On Device, then tap the app that you want to view. Sort the apps in your library with the sort options to the right of the Navigation Panel button in the upper left corner. Sort options include by recent and title.

If you delete a purchased app from your HDX, it still exists in the cloud, and can be re-downloaded at any time by going to your Apps from the Navigation Bar, then tapping the Cloud option, then tapping the app you want to re-download.

Apps that you recently purchased or used are displayed in your Carousel, and can be removed from the Carousel by tapping and holding on them and then choosing the Remove from Carousel option. To remove a purchased app from your app library, tap and hold on the title and then select the Remove from Device option.

Email & Calendar

Email Account Setup

Email is one thing the HDX does frightfully well, and you'll want to set it up to check your email if at all possible. Depending on what service you use for your emails, you may have to tweak some settings around to get it working properly, but in general, the following instructions should work for both large services (like Gmail) and self-hosted mail.

To start, open the Email app from the Home Screen or from the Apps section of the Navigation Bar. You'll see something like this once you do:

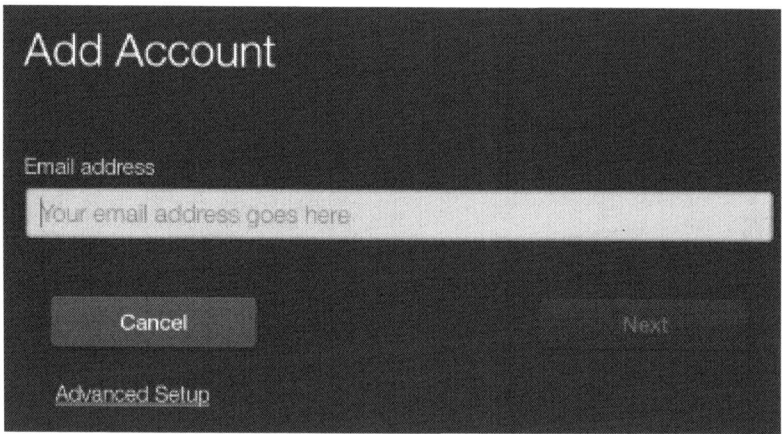

Type in your email address and tap Next to get to the next screen. From here, enter your password and tap Next again. If your email account was auto-configured, congrats! You're set to go with no further configuration needed.

If it wasn't auto-configured (which is likely if you're self-hosting your email), you'll need to do a bit more to finish the setup. Tap Advanced Setup and select your server type, then enter in your email server information as requested. This advanced information may not be readily available to you unless you're familiar with server/email administration, so you may need to contact your email provider for this information.

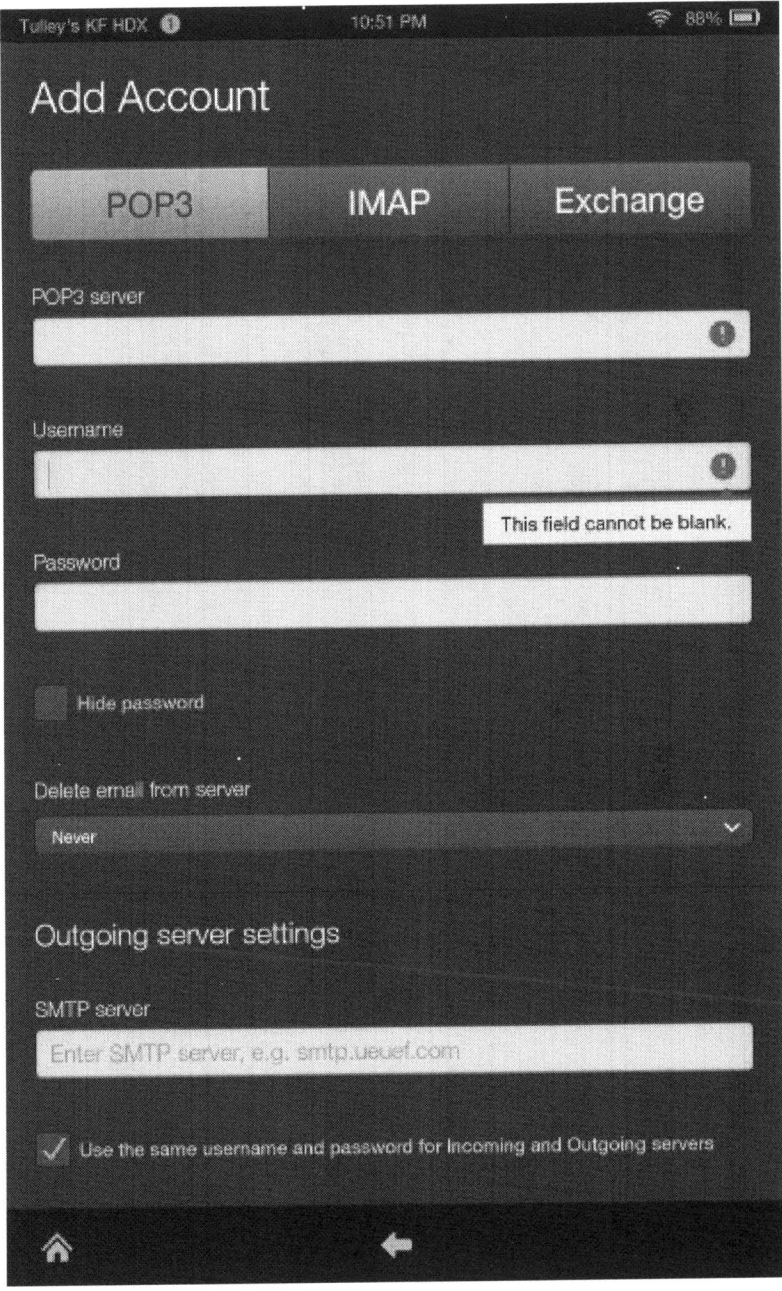

Once your account is configured either automatically or through the advanced setup screen, tap the Next button and you'll be ready to go.

Once you're viewing the inbox for your newly created email account, open the Navigation Panel (swipe from the left to right from the edge of the screen or tap the Nav Panel button in the upper lefthand corner of the screen) and then tap Settings. From here, you can change Email, Contacts and Calendar settings, as well as specific account settings. You can also add a new account here as well.

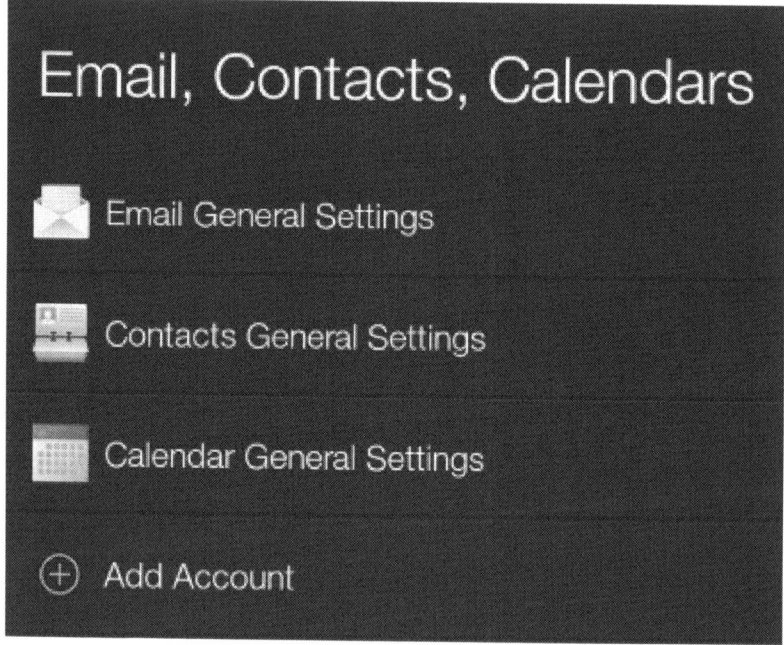

Remove Email Account

From your inbox in the Email app, open the Navigation Panel, tap Settings and then tap on the account name that you want to remove. At the very bottom of the menu that appears, tap the Remove Account option and confirm the removal of the email account from your HDX.

Change Email Account Settings

From your inbox in the Email app, open the Navigation Panel, tap Settings and then tap on the account name that you want to modify. From here, you'll see a screen like this appear:

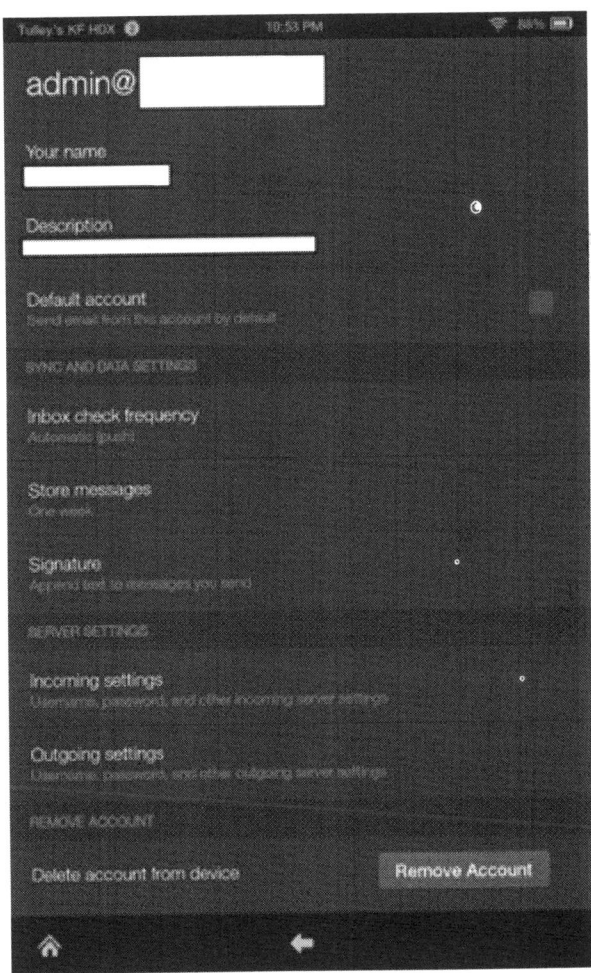

From here you can tap on any of the options to change them, starting with changing how your name appears on outgoing emails to the incoming and outgoing server settings for the account.

TV, Video, Audiobooks & Music

Buying/Renting TV & Movies

From the Home screen, tap the Videos button in the Navigation Bar to open the default view of the Amazon Video store, which will look something like this:

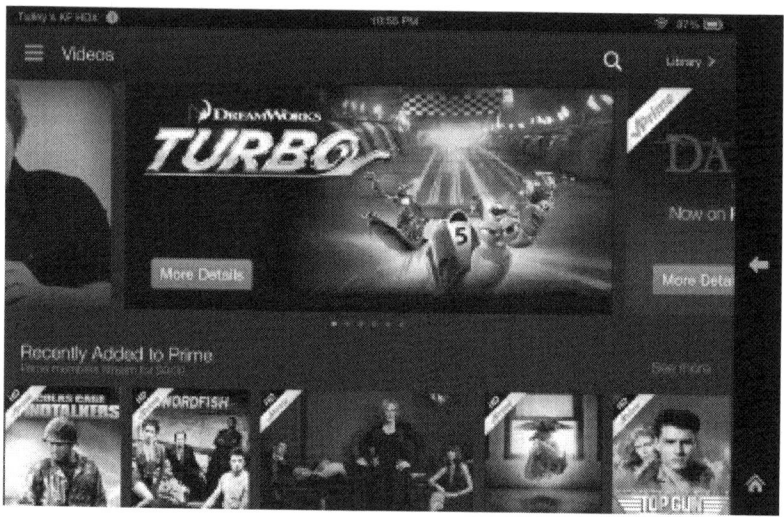

From here, you can open the Navigation Panel (swipe from the left edge of the screen or tap the button in the upper left corner) to navigate through various categories and genres of TV shows and movies, or you can swipe up and down or left and right in the list of videos to see what's new and popular.

Tapping on a video will take you to the details page for that video, where you'll have the option to purchase it or, in some cases, to rent it for a short period of time for a cheaper price. Videos that you purchase or rent can either be streamed to your HDX to view, or you can choose to download them.

If you download a video that you purchase or rent, you can access it by tapping the Library button in the upper right corner of the Videos screen, then choosing either Cloud (to view all of your rented/purchased videos) or On Device (to view all of your downloaded videos). Tap the Store button in the upper right of the screen to go back to the Store.

Don't forget that you can tap the Search icon in the Options Bar to perform searches for specific movies or TV shows in addition to browsing through the genres in the Navigation Panel.

Finding Amazon Prime Videos

If you have an Amazon Prime subscription, you'll have access to thousands of movies and TV shows that you can stream (but not download) free of charge. You can identify these free videos by the Prime badge on them:

Note that these videos can't be downloaded, but you can stream them to watch them as many times as you want, both on your Kindle and through your web browser, for as long as your Prime account is active and for as long as Amazon provides access to the videos.

Music & Audiobooks

If you've read the above sections on how to purchase movies and TV shows, then you're well-prepared to purchase music and audiobooks as well. To get started, just tap on the appropriate button on the Navigation Bar to access your Music or Audiobook library.

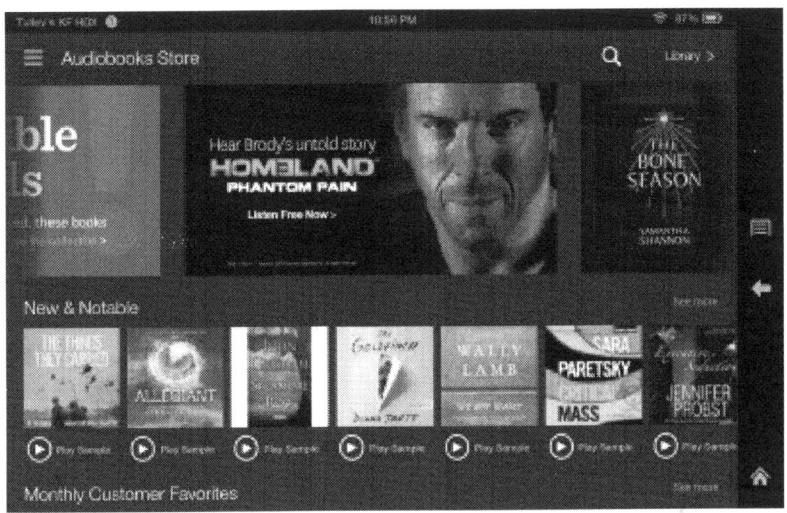

From here, tap the Store button in the upper right corner. Then, just like you would see when purchasing movies, TV shows, books or apps, you'll see all of the music and audiobooks available for purchase from Amazon. Like other digital products, when you purchase audio products, they're automatically downloaded to your HDX and stored in your local library. And, if you delete them from your device, you can re-download them at any time from the Cloud section of your library.

Audiobooks have another neat feature, though. Many books have professionally recorded audiobooks that go along with them, and if you purchase both the book and the audiobook, you can read the book and listen to it in tandem. Using Whispersync technology, your audio progress and reading progress are synced, so you can switch back and forth between reading and listening to your book all without losing your place.

Taking & Editing Pictures & Videos

Photo/Video Basics

Tap the Photos button in the Navigation Bar to open the photo/video section of your HDX. From here, you can swipe through to view photos and videos you've taken. Tap on a photo or video to either view it full-screen or play it, or swipe from the left (or tap the Navigation Panel button in the upper left corner) to view the filter options.

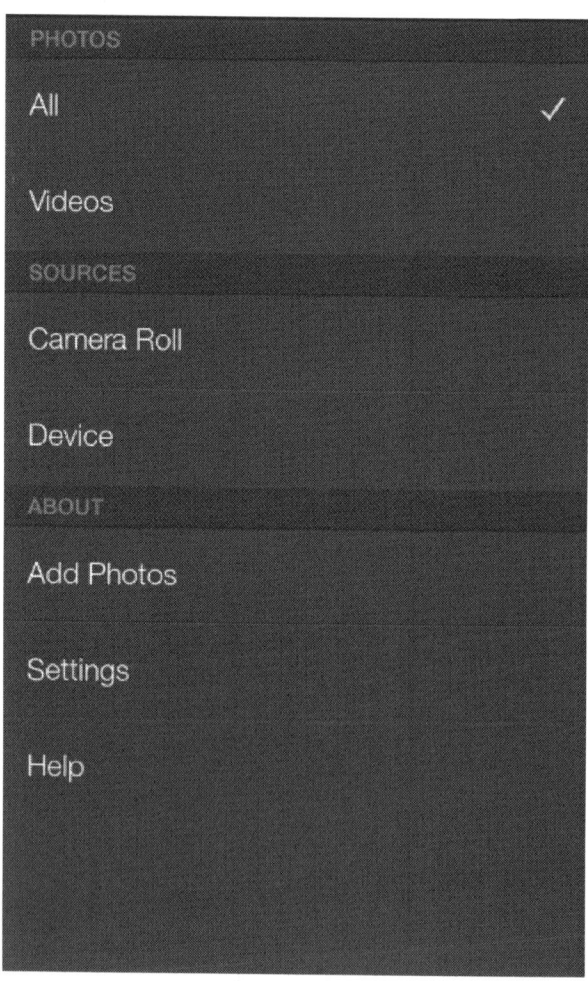

Tap on the types of media you want to display in the photo library, select a source to view or tap the Settings button to turn on Cloud Storage backup for your photos. This option will save your photos to your Amazon Cloud drive so that they're backed up even if you delete them from the device.

When viewing a photo or video in full screen, tap the center of the screen to reveal the options bars, then tap the back button to return to the photo library.

From the main photo library, you can also tap the share button (

) to share a photo with someone in your social media groups, or you can use an app like Email to share the photo. Tap the options

button ( ) to delete, edit or view information on the photo you are viewing.

From the photo library, you can also tap and hold on a photo or video to open a popup to share, edit, view info about or delete the photo or video you are viewing.

Taking Pictures/Videos

If you want to take a picture or video, tap the camera button ( ). This opens up the camera app. Tap the Camera/Video button

( ) to switch between camera and video mode. Tap the

shutter/record button ( ) to take a picture or start/stop recording a video, tap the back button to return to the photo library or

tap the gallery button ( ) to view the Camera Roll (a list of photos/videos you've taken sorted by date).

Please note that only the 8.9" Kindle Fire HDX features dual cameras (one forward and one rear facing); the 7" HDX model only features a single camera.

Photo Editing

Basic photo editing functionality is provided by tapping and holding on a photo in the gallery and selecting the edit button, or from individual photos by tapping on the options button and choosing the edit option.

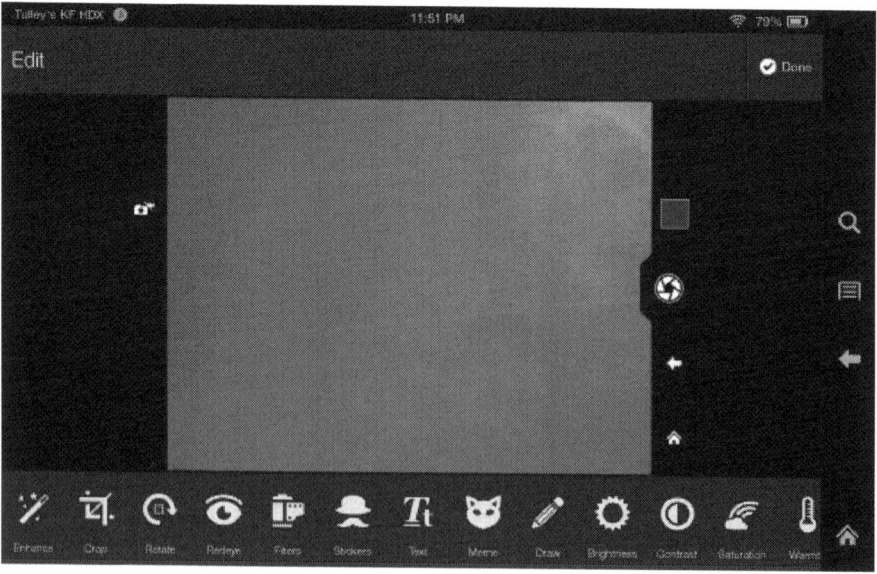

Using the editing functions at the bottom of the screen, you can enhance, crop, rotate, remove redeye and perform more editing functions on your photos. Be sure to swipe back and forth on the functions at the bottom to view the full list, as there's quite a few! Once you've finished editing your photo, tap the Done button at the top to save your changes.

Note that at the time of writing, no video editing functionality is provided by the Kindle Fire HDX out of the box.

Advanced Settings, Tips & Tricks

So, what's left to cover? We've gone through pretty much everything except the huge amount of settings in the Settings section of the Quick Settings menu (swipe down from the top of the screen to access Quick Settings).

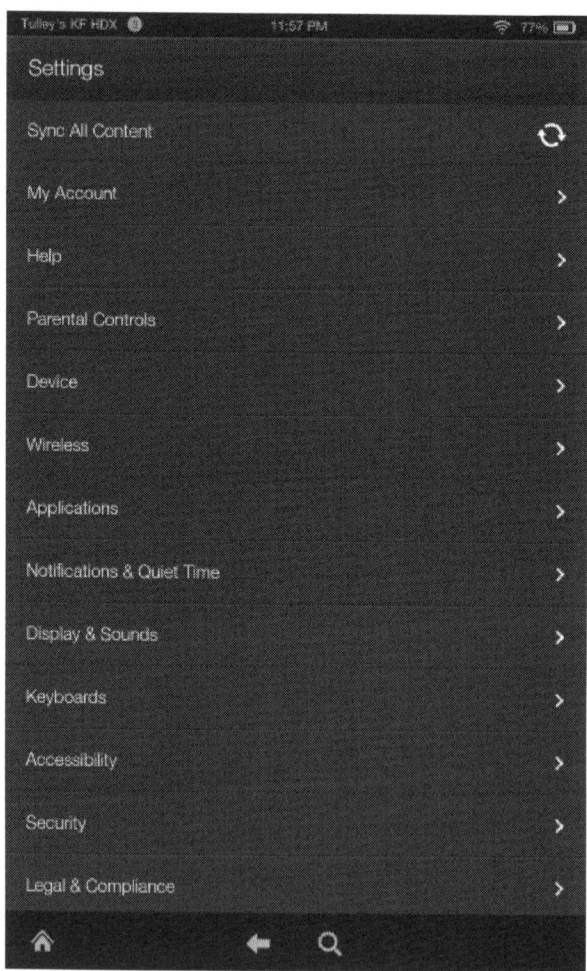

These settings let you change so many things about your HDX, so I'm going to explain what all of those settings mean and what they do for you right here, right now. Afterward, I'll go through a few tips and tricks I've learned from my years as a Kindle Fire Expert that should help you with your new HDX. Let's get started!

My Account

I won't be showing a screenshot of this section for privacy reasons, but here's where you can see (and change) what Amazon account your HDX is registered to, what your HDX's assigned @kindle.com email address is (for emailing files to your HDX, as covered earlier in this guide book) and view/change your Amazon settings. These include your account settings, your country settings, payment options, subscriptions and, last but not least, manage your social media connections that you've established.

Help

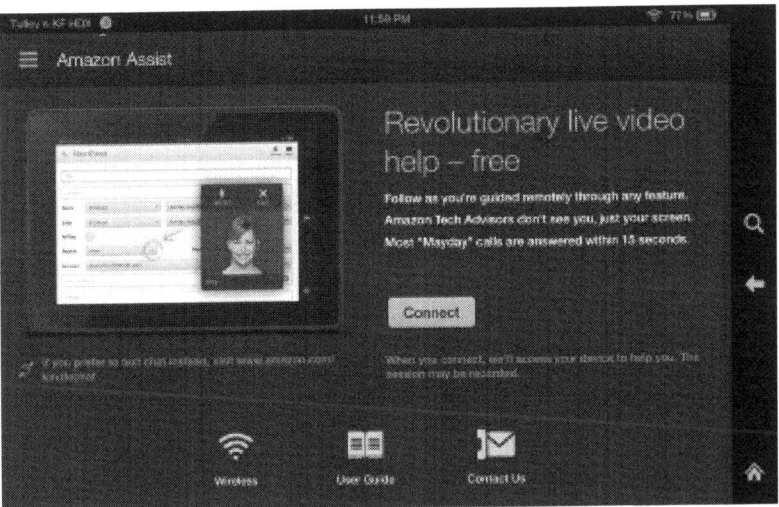

Ah, the good old Help section! This section was covered earlier in this guide book, but in summary, you can access Mayday, wireless setup guides, the HDX user guide and contact information for Amazon from this section.

Parental Controls

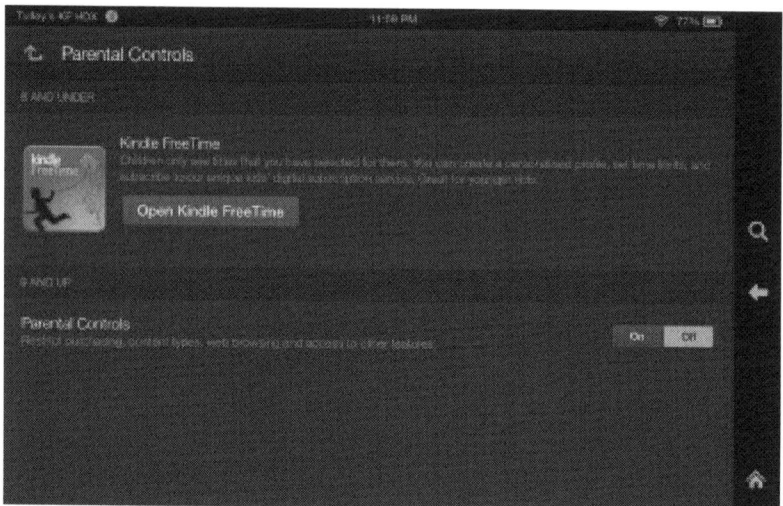

Want to manage how your children (or other adults, for that matter!) access your HDX? This is the section where you can restrict what they can and can't access (such as turning off web browser and app purchasing abilities) and how much time they're allowed to spend on the Kindle.

Device

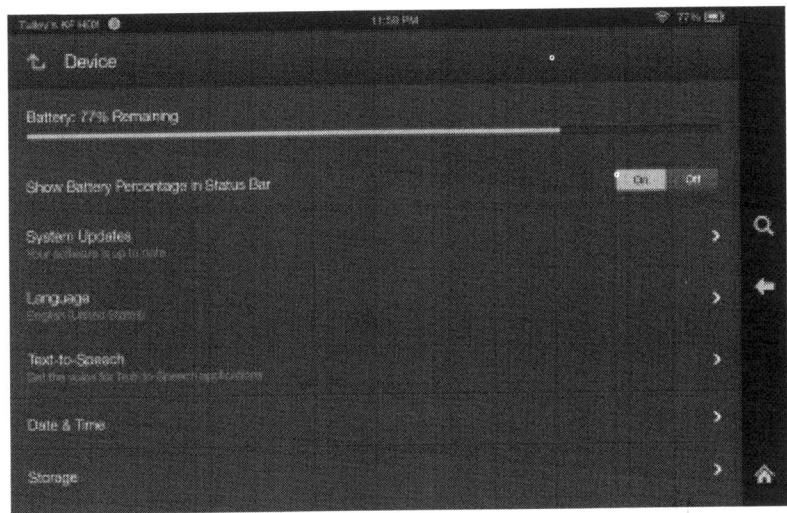

Here you'll find your current battery charge, choose whether you want the total battery percentage remaining to be displayed in the Notification/Status Bar, perform system updates, change the language on your Kindle HDX, choose what applications you want to use text-to-speech with, set the date and time, view and manage the storage space taken up by files and apps and enable ADB debugging. ADB debugging is generally only used by developers, so it's a good idea to leave this setting turned to the off position.

This is also the section where you can perform a factory default reset on your Kindle Fire HDX. Note that doing so will permanently erase all data stored locally on your HDX (but will not delete Amazon-purchased digital content, as that data is stored in the Cloud) including locally stored/loaded files, settings, photos/videos, applications and more.

Wireless

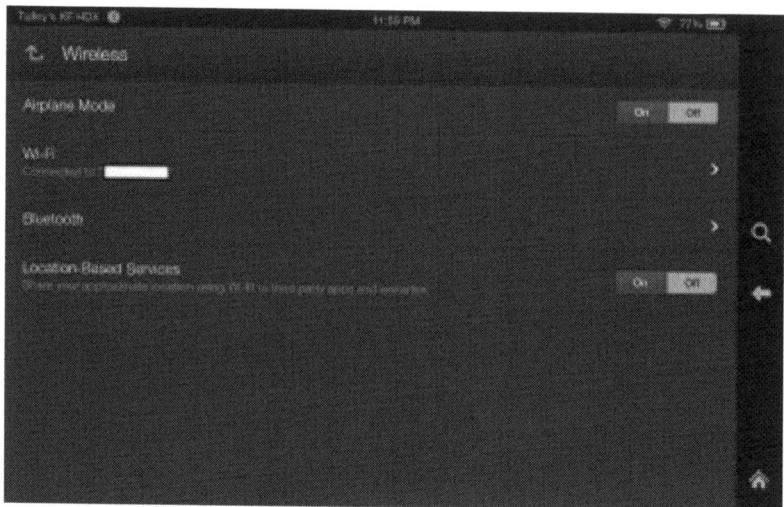

As we discussed early in this guide book, the Wireless section gives you access to all of your Wi-Fi and Bluetooth settings, as well as cell network (4G) settings, if you have an HDX with 4G capabilities. For more info on this section, turn to the beginning of the book where I went over the wireless settings options.

Applications

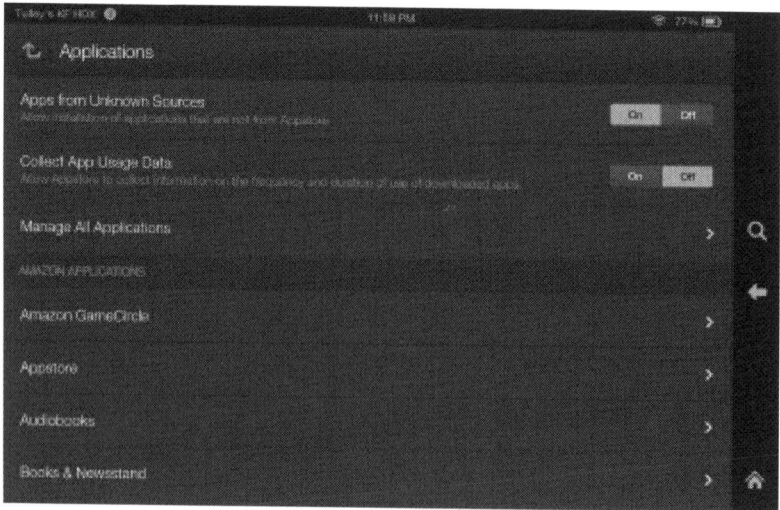

In order to side-load apps (which we'll cover a few sections down), you'll need to turn on the Apps from Unknown Sources option found in this section. Here you can also choose whether you want to send anonymous data about your app usage to Amazon.

If an app gets stuck or stops responding, you can go into Manage All Applications, tap on the app that's misbehaving and choose the Force Stop option. This could cause data loss, so use caution! You can also view and clear information about apps in this section, so use caution with that, too!

For all of the Amazon apps (camera, music, photos, audiobooks, etc.) the individual settings for each one are found in this section. For example, under the Camera section you can choose whether to have Location Tags enabled, and under the Music section you can choose whether you want newly purchased music to automatically download to your HDX and you can clear any cached songs on your HDX that were stored during streaming sessions. Explore the options in these sections with caution, since changing even one can have a major impact on how your HDX operates.

Notifications & Quiet Time

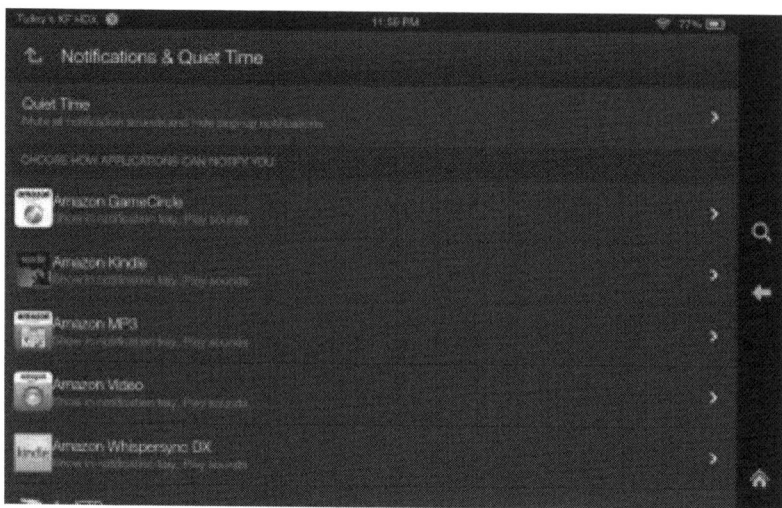

The Quick Settings menu gives you access to Quiet Time, which you can also access in this section. Quiet Time, when enabled, will mute all notifications on your HDX. From this settings section, you can also set up a Quiet Time schedule (perfect for if you get a lot of emails at night when you're trying to sleep, like me).

You'll also be able to configure how each application on your HDX is allowed to notify you, both by notifications in the notification tray and by playing sounds. Simply tap the app whose notification settings you want to change and turn notifications on or off.

Display & Sounds

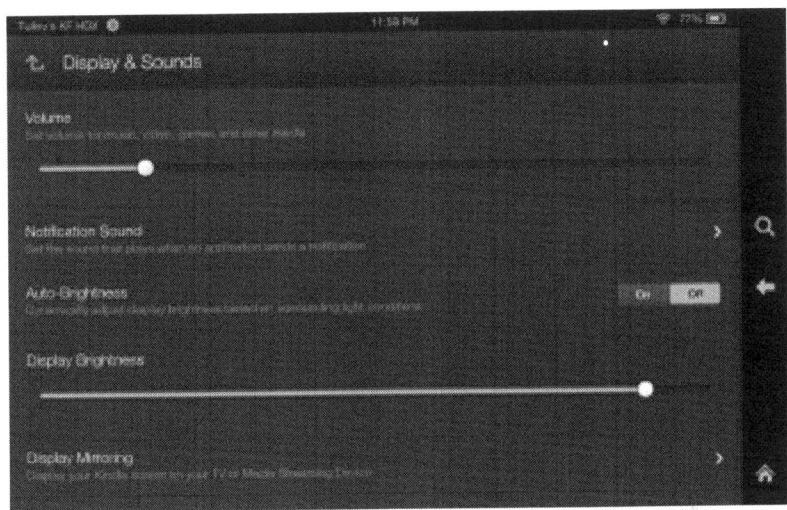

Change the master volume for the system here, as well as what sound you want to hear when the HDX has a notification for you. You can also turn auto-brightness on or off here as well as adjust the display brightness in general. If you have connected your HDX to a TV or media streaming device, you can mirror the HDX's display to that device here as well. Finally, you can adjust how long the HDX waits before going to sleep and turning the screen off in this section. The default is five minutes, but choosing a shorter period may help to conserve battery life, depending on how you use your HDX.

Keyboards

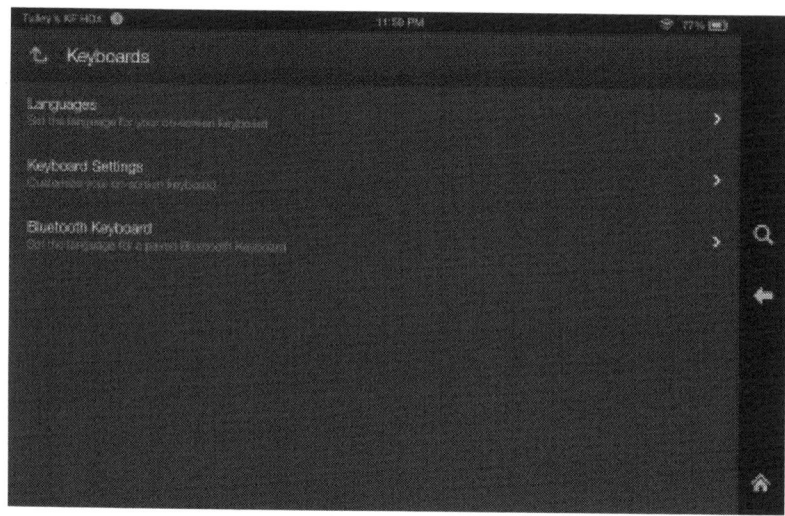

If you want to change the language for your on-screen keyboard, you can do so here. This is also where you can change your Keyboard settings to make sounds when you touch keys, turn spelling auto-correction on or off, turn automatic capitalization on or off, turn on or off word prediction (tries to guess what word you'll type next based on what you've already typed in an effort to save you time), turn spell checking on or off and, finally, where you can view what words you've added to your personal dictionary so that even if the HDX thinks that you've made a horrible spelling mistake, it'll stop bugging you about it. (No, HDX, "Tulley" is *not*, contrary to your opinion, a spelling mistake.)

If you've paired up a keyboard via Bluetooth to your HDX, here's where you'll be able to fine-tune the settings for that, as well.

Accessibility

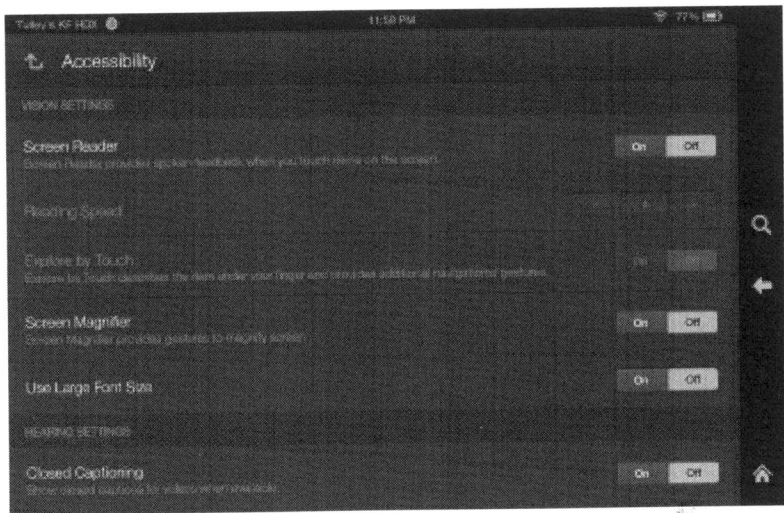

Need some spoken help when you touch things on the screen? Or do you need a screen magnifier that will zoom in when you swipe in certain ways? Options for those with vision or hearing problems are found here, along with a comprehensive user guide for configuring these options.

Security

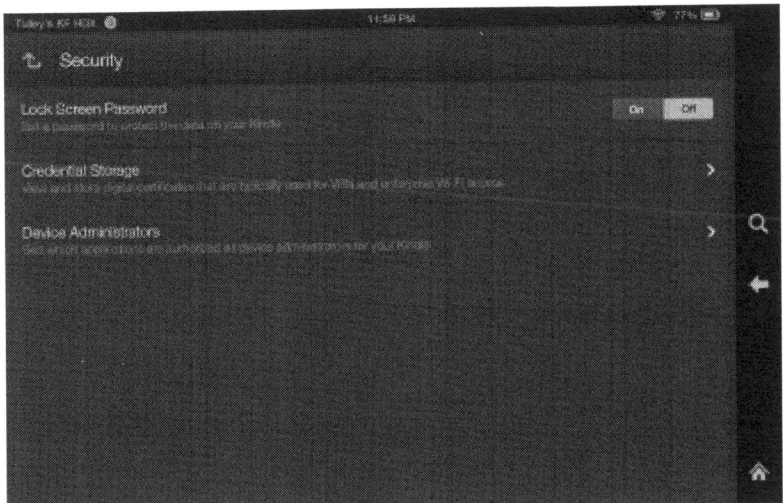

Here's where you can set up a password so that when your HDX wakes up from sleep, it takes more than a quick swipe to access your data. Be sure to remember your password, though, since if you forget it, you may have to contact Amazon Customer Service to get it fixed. This is also the section where you can store VPN certificates and give or set information to and from device administrators. Home users won't have to worry about these sections, though, so don't fret if you don't know what this means, as these settings are pretty much always and only used in business environments.

Legal & Compliance

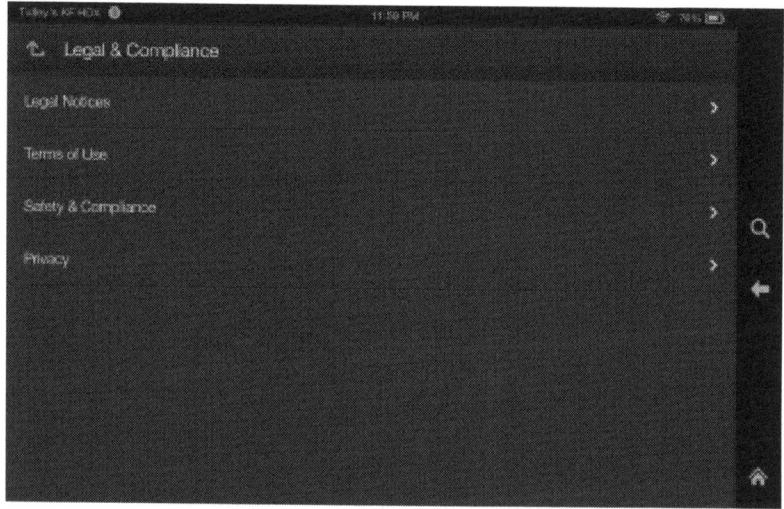

Unless you're a lawyer or just love to read pages of legalese, you won't find anything in here that's very interesting. Amazon's terms and conditions, privacy policies and other legal notices are contained in this section, which is—thankfully—at the very bottom of the list of settings. I've opened it once by accident and don't intend to do so again.

Tips & Tricks

Reset to Factory Defaults

To reset your HDX back to how it was when it arrived from Amazon, swipe open the Quick Settings menu, tap Settings, tap Device and then tap Reset to Factory Defaults and confirm the operation. Your HDX will reset at least once during this operation, so don't try to power it on or off until the operation is complete. Note that performing this reset operation will permanently erase all data stored locally on your HDX (but will not delete Amazon-purchased digital content, as that data is stored in the Cloud) including locally stored/loaded files, settings, photos/videos, applications and more.

Side Loading Apps

Side loading is the fancy name for installing apps on your HDX from sources other than the Amazon Appstore. If you have an app that you want to install saved to your HDX (in the file format of a .APK file), use a file explorer program (I recommend ES File Explorer in my Best 100 Kindle Fire HDX Apps book) to browse to the APK file, then tap on it to install it. (Note that in the screenshots below, I've censored out the names of certain apps that I've purchased and backed up to avoid copyright issues.)

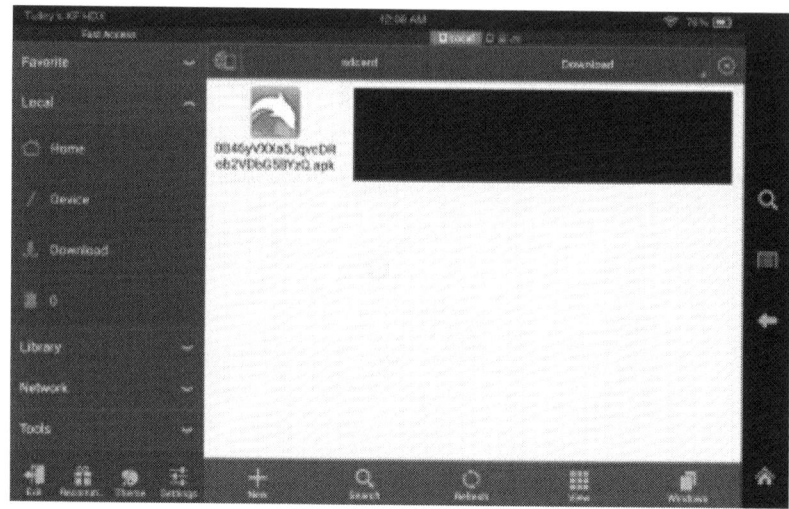

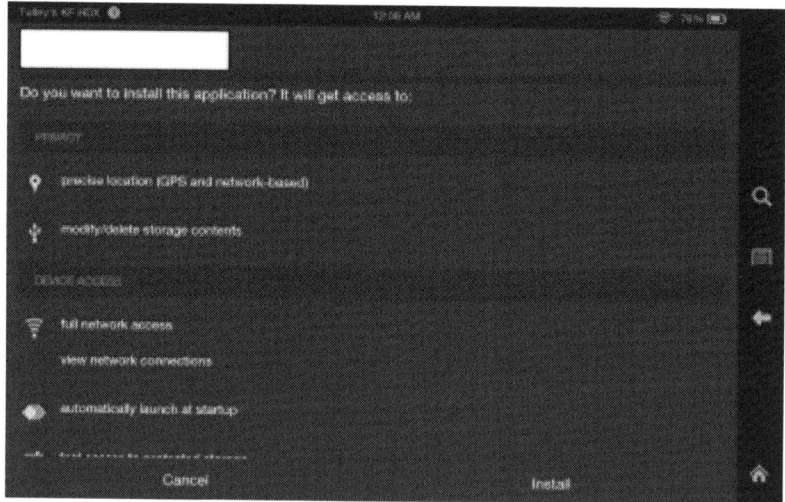

Before you can side-load apps, though, you'll have to change a security setting on your HDX. See, the underlying Android operating system on the HDX doesn't like to have unauthorized apps install themselves on your system, so the ability to do so is turned off by default. Swipe down to access the Quick Settings menu, then tap Settings, then tap Applications. Change the option for Apps from Unknown Sources from Off to On, and confirm the change. Once you do so, you'll be able to side-load apps as described above.

Viewing Adobe Flash Content

Adobe stopped supporting Flash on Android devices over a year ago, but Amazon's picked up where they left off in the Silk browser. Without having to side-load any additional apps, you can use the Silk browser's Experimental Streaming Viewer to watch and interact with Flash-based content. Doing so is simple, but you need to ensure that the Prompt for Experimental Streaming Viewer option on the browser is checked. Then, when you visit a page that contains Flash content, the browser will ask you if you want to try and load the page with the Experimental Streaming Viewer. Tap to indicate in the affirmative, and the page will reload, and the Flash content will be viewable.

Taking Screenshots

Taking screenshots is easy on your Kindle Fire HDX! Just press and hold the power and volume down buttons at the same time for a few seconds until the screen flashes, and presto! The screenshot is taken and stored in your photo library for quick and easy viewing.

More Tips & Tricks

For more tips and tricks, visit www.appsna.gr/hdxtips to sign up for the Kindle Fire HDX newsletter. I've partnered with AppSnagr to send this newsletter out 1-2 times per week, and it's chock-full of awesome HDX information, app recommendations, book recommendations and more! Best of all, this information is constantly updated, so you'll always have the latest info right at your fingertips!

Physical Care of Your New Kindle Fire HDX

When you use your Kindle Fire HDX, you should take care of it like you would any other semi-fragile electronic device. You don't necessarily need to baby it, but you should protect it from big dangers.

Food & Drink

For example, don't eat or drink near your Kindle Fire HDX, as any drinks or food spilled on it could cause irreparable harm. If you absolutely must eat or drink near your Kindle Fire HDX, use caution, and try not to hold or move food or drink over the device to minimize the risk of spilling anything on it.

Cleaning the Screen & Body

The screen of your Kindle Fire HDX is tough, but not invulnerable. I personally don't use a screen protector on my Kindle Fire HDX because it rarely leaves my desk or a custom cloth pouch I made for it, but a screen protect is an excellent way to keep the screen from getting scratched or marred.

If you don't apply a screen protector, you can clean the screen of your Kindle Fire HDX with a microfiber cloth. Just turn the screen off, gently remove any large pieces of dust or dirt (to keep from scratching the screen), then just wipe the screen with the microfiber until clean. You can use this same cloth to clean the rest of the body of the device, too.

Watch the Temperature

When you watch videos or play games on your Kindle Fire HDX, the device can get very warm. It has no cooling fans on it, so it relies on passive cooling to keep from overheating. If you're doing a media-intensive task for a long period of time, make sure that the device has plenty of space around it to cool off. Also, don't let it run in direct sunlight, as sunlight on the black surface of the device will cause it to heat up even faster. I'd personally recommend removing it from any protective cases (unless they have ventilation holes or they're thin enough to let heat pass through them at a rapid rate) while playing games or watching movies, but I'm a bit overly cautious with my device.

That's All, Folks!

If you've gotten this far, then you know how to do so many things with your Kindle Fire HDX! I hope you've learned a lot and that this book has been helpful to you.

Last updated at the end of 2014, this paperback copy of the Kindle Fire HDX User Guide should remain relevant for some time. To ensure you're kept up to speed with any major changes Amazon makes to the HDX, though, be sure to re-visit Amazon and pick up the Kindle version of this user guide.

Updated monthly, the Kindle version of the HDX user guide will contain information on the changes that Amazon makes, and is often available at a severely discounted price.

Don't forget to check out my other book, **Best 100 Kindle Fire HDX Apps**. For $0.99 it's the best resource for finding my favorite apps on the Amazon Appstore to help you be productive and have more fun with your Kindle fire HDX.

Made in the USA
Lexington, KY
08 October 2015